Hometown Heroes

Hometown Heroes

Real Stories of Ordinary People Doing Extraordinary Things All Across America

An American Profile Book

Edited by Marta Warnick Aldrich, Stuart Englert, and Richard McVey

Foreword by Philip Gulley

HarperSanFrancisco
A Division of HarperCollins*Publishers*

HarperCollins books may be purchased for educational, business, or sales promotional use. For information please write: Special Markets Department, HarperCollins Publishers, 10 East 53rd Street, New York, NY 10022.

American Profile Web site: americanprofile.com
HarperCollins Web site: http://www.harpercollins.com
HarperCollins®, ®, and HarperSanFrancisco™
are trademarks of HarperCollins Publishers.

FIRST EDITION
Designed by Joseph Rutt
Maps by Topaz Maps, Inc.

Library of Congress Cataloging-in-Publication Data
is available upon request.

ISBN: 978–0–06–125238–9
ISBN-10: 0–06–125238–7

07 08 09 10 11 RRD(H) 10 9 8 7 6 5 4 3 2

Contents

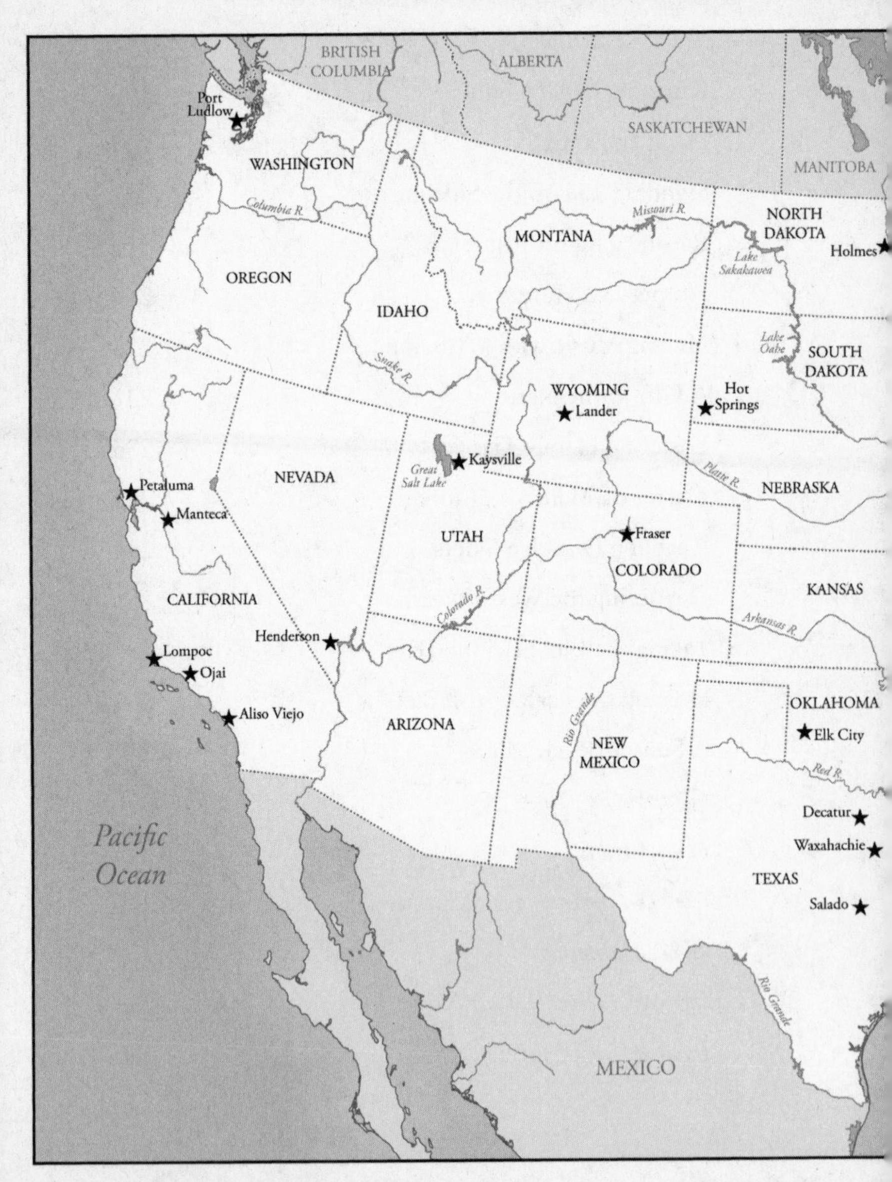

BRITISH COLUMBIA
ALBERTA
SASKATCHEWAN
MANITOBA
Port Ludlow
WASHINGTON
Columbia R.
Missouri R.
NORTH DAKOTA
Holmes
MONTANA
Lake Sakakawea
OREGON
IDAHO
Lake Oahe
SOUTH DAKOTA
Snake R.
WYOMING
Lander
Hot Springs
Kaysville
Great Salt Lake
Platte R.
NEBRASKA
Petaluma
NEVADA
Manteca
Fraser
UTAH
COLORADO
KANSAS
CALIFORNIA
Colorado R.
Arkansas R.
Henderson
Lompoc
Ojai
OKLAHOMA
Aliso Viejo
Rio Grande
ARIZONA
Elk City
NEW MEXICO
Red R.
Decatur
Pacific Ocean
Waxahachie
TEXAS
Salado
Rio Grande
MEXICO

PRINCE EDWARD ISLAND
NEW BRUNSWICK
NOVA SCOTIA
QUEBEC
ONTARIO
Lake Nipigon
Lake Superior
MAINE
VT
NH
Hudson
MA
CT
RI
NEW YORK
MINNESOTA
Zimmerman
Delano
Shakopee
Suamico
Neenah
WISCONSIN
Lake Michigan
Lake Huron
Lake Ontario
Lake Erie
Saginaw
MICHIGAN
Portage
Hastings-on-Hudson
Wesport
Forest Hills
Pittstown
NJ
Middlefield
PENNSYLVANIA
IOWA
Earlham
ILLINOIS
Ellisville
INDIANA
Bellville
OHIO
Mt. Morris
Cape May
DE
MD
Danville
North Vernon
Ohio R.
Louisville
WEST VIRGINIA
VIRGINIA
Valley Falls
Paxico
MISSOURI
Halfway
KENTUCKY
Belhaven
Norris
NORTH CAROLINA
Grove
Sperry
TENNESSEE
Parsons
Mississippi R.
ARKANSAS
SOUTH CAROLINA
Marietta
Moody
ALABAMA
GEORGIA
MISSISSIPPI
Hilton Head Island
Atlantic Ocean
LOUISIANA
FLORIDA
Clermont
Ocean Breeze Park
Gulf of Mexico

Foreword

Those of us who make our living with words are especially sensitive to their use, and misuse. Perhaps overly so. Several years ago, I noticed our growing fascination with the word *hero.* Heroes used to be people who sacrificed their lives for the sake of someone else. They tended to congregate in certain places—fire stations, police stations, civil rights marches, and battlefields. Now heroes are everywhere, thicker than fleas, being cited for, well, for just being. I recently was in a first-grade classroom and overheard a teacher tell her pupils they were her heroes.

"I'm all for self-esteem," I complained to my wife that evening, "but when twenty kids are heroes just for tying their shoes, where does that leave a Medal of Honor winner?"

My wife is accustomed to my rantings on matters of language, and she suggested I take a softer line. "How come when men hear the word *hero*, they think of General Patton or Superman? How about the parents who scrape by and do without, so their kids can go to college? Or folks who give up their vacation to build houses for poor people? That's pretty heroic."

My wife is right a lot more often than I am.

You won't find any Medal of Honor winners in this book, no Supermen or Wonder Women. But you will find Anthony Leanna of Suamico, Wisconsin, who at the age of 10 began collecting hats for cancer patients made bald by chemotherapy. He formed a non-profit organization called Heavenly Hats and within five years had given away 102,000 hats to cancer patients in 275 hospitals around the country. He's 15 now, and still at it.

Heroism isn't just for the young. Consider Dorothy Geeben of Ocean Breeze Park, Florida, who at the age of 94 was elected mayor of her town. In her spare time, she revived a church that had dwindled to one member—her. She found a minister, hired him, got to working, and helped the congregation grow a hundred-fold, to 100 members. Now 99, she still is the mayor, still shows up for work and still too busy to appear with Jay Leno on *The Tonight Show* when he phoned to invite her.

I guess what some heroes teach us is that we're never too young or too old to be of help to someone else.

There are fifty heroes in this little book. Fifty stories of ordinary folks who woke up one morning and decided to do something with their lives. One of them built a library for her small Illinois town, another became a Santa and learned sign language so deaf children could sit on Santa's lap too. One woman devoted her life to making farm life safer for children after her 11-year-old son was crushed under tons of corn.

We have grown accustomed in this country to looking in the wrong places for leadership and vision. Washington, D.C., and Hollywood are interesting places to visit, but not very good incubators for inspiration. For that we need to look to Shakopee, Minnesota, to Barbara Hensley, who is taking on the scourge of breast cancer. Personally, I don't think breast cancer stands a chance.

If your faith in humanity has sagged, this book is for you. Enjoy it slowly, like a box of fine chocolates, savoring one story at a time. I'll make no bold claim. It probably won't change your life. But it will cause you to remember the Light of Human Goodness that still cuts through the gloom. And these days, that's no small thing.

—PHILIP GULLEY

Lake Michigan
Ellisville
ILLINOIS
Population: 87
Chicago
ILLINOIS
HELEN MYERS

Little Library, Big Heart

At 9 A.M. on Saturday, Helen Myers troops four blocks to the little library in Ellisville, Illinois, and unlocks the door. She hoists the flag outside, then settles down with a good book and waits for company.

"If I have two people come in, it's a big crowd," says Myers, 79.

The great-grandmother could write a book on patience and dedication. For more than 40 years, she's kept the library humming, spending 37 of those years in a dilapidated shed-sized building. Since 2003, however, her library has resided in a tidy new building built on faith, donations, and old-fashioned sugar cookies.

It all began in 1966, when Myers opened her library with 400 books from her home shelves at the prompting of a grade-school boy in the community service group she was shepherding. "He noticed that I had a lot of books, and he said, 'I sure wish we could have a library here in town,'" Myers recalls. That's all the motivation the bookworm needed.

"I can't remember ever not reading," says Myers, who was raised in Ellisville and taught school one year there at age 18 with an emergency teaching license issued during World War II. During her life, she's worked as a wallpaper hanger and secretary and has been the village treasurer for 32 years.

"If you can read, you can do anything," Myers declares. "Today, though, people don't read. They watch TV and play those darn video games."

That hasn't discouraged her from faithfully opening the library from 9 to 11 A.M. on Saturdays to share her love of literature. One of her favorite books is Jack London's *Call of the Wild*, which she read four times in high school. She prefers nonfiction, though, and is continuously reading two biographies or self-help books at home and two at the library.

"When you consider the size of this town, it's pretty amazing what Helen has done," says Bonnie Powell, who has worked alongside her friend for more than 20 years in the Ellisville Goal Getters. The town's mothers organized in 1983 to build a basketball court, and they've been holding monthly fund-raising feeds ever since.

The library, though, has always been Myers's pet project. In the 1970s, when the roof and floor rotted beyond repair in the donated 10-by-14-foot building, she began saving dollars for a new structure.

The foundation was built from sales of sugar cookies. Myers rolls out the giant 50-cent cookies on the first two weekends in October during the area's Spoon River Valley Scenic Drive fall festival. The event brings visitors from miles around to Ellisville and to the library's front door in search of Myers's homemade cookies. She bakes and decorates about six dozen shaped like Fulton County, and they're bestsellers. The cookie money now helps pay the library's utility bills.

As publicity spread about the state's tiniest library, donations started coming in. First lady Laura Bush, a former librarian, sent seven books and a note congratulating her on her dedication in maintaining a library in such a small town.

With $8,000 in donations, cookie sales, and her own savings, Myers built Ellisville Library II, which opened October 26, 2003, on her own property, four blocks from her house. The building, with white siding and green trim, is 14 feet by 22 feet and stacked with 3,500 donated hardbacks, new and used.

Displayed atop the children's bookshelf are new Harry Potter books. Fiction is arranged alphabetically by authors' names, and nonfiction is grouped by subject. Baskets on the floor hold free paperbacks.

No fines are charged because that would discourage reading. "I've had some books overdue since 1981," Myers says with a laugh.

Only 20 books are ever in circulation at one time, and most weeks Myers opens and closes the library and never sees a soul.

"My daughter said, 'Mom, why don't you give it up and close up?'" Myers relates. "I said, 'No. Somebody, some day, may read. Who knows? A future president of the United States may come in and get a book.'"

—Marti Attoun

Be patient and faithful in all you do. Patience is an often overlooked virtue.

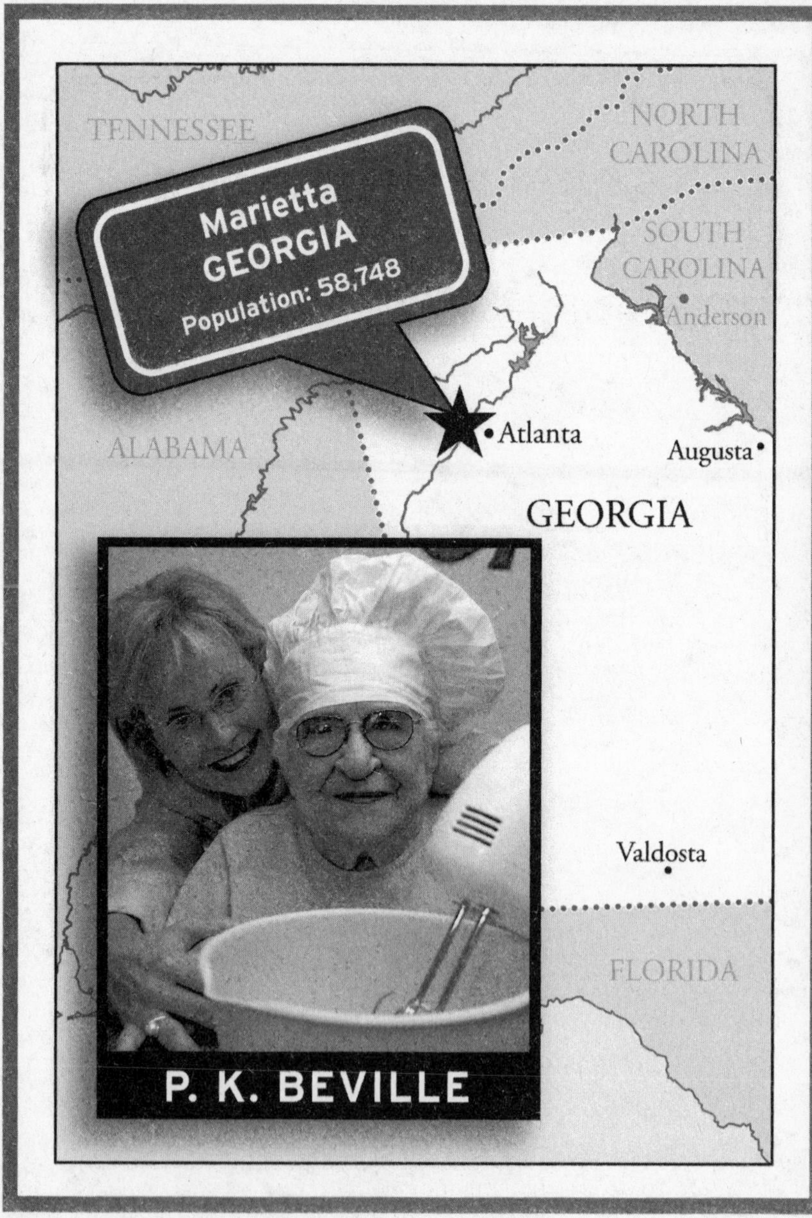

TENNESSEE

NORTH CAROLINA

Marietta
GEORGIA
Population: 58,748

SOUTH CAROLINA

Anderson

ALABAMA

Atlanta

Augusta

GEORGIA

Valdosta

FLORIDA

P. K. BEVILLE

Angel to the Aged

P. K. Beville is a dream come true for elders living in nursing homes and assisted living centers. Since 1997, the Marietta, Georgia, woman has helped thousands of senior citizens realize their dreams, from riding a roller coaster to being reunited with a long-lost family member.

"A dream can be as simple as a new dress," says Beville, 54, founder and CEO of Second Wind Dreams, a nonprofit organization whose mission is to let seniors know how special they are. "People in eldercare facilities usually can't run out to a Macy's sale like the rest of us."

A geriatrics specialist for more than 20 years, Beville used to perform psychological evaluations of residents of long-term care facilities. During those evaluations, residents often spoke longingly about their desire to dance, visit an old home town, or even just to cook again, and Beville wondered why someone didn't make those things happen. Finally, she stopped wondering and started Second Wind Dreams in the basement of her home.

Since then, Beville and thousands of volunteers and employees of nursing homes and assisted living centers have taken elders for blimp rides and to Disney World and have taught several seniors to swim. They arranged for an Illinois senior to ride a camel, an 86-year-old West Virginia woman to direct an orchestra, and a life-long golf fan to play in the PGA Senior Golf Tournament. They took a New York man to a NASCAR race, sent one couple on a Hawaiian cruise to celebrate more than 50 years of marriage, and arranged for a 91-year-old woman to go ballroom dancing. On average, Second Wind fulfills three dreams a day and has served people in 41 states and two foreign countries.

Often, the dreams are quite simple—things like going on a picnic, hearing a live choir sing, or riding in a red convertible on a sunny day. In 2005, Second Wind fulfilled Pollyanna Birchfield's desire to bake one last cake. Birchfield, then 87 and a resident of the A. G. Rhodes Home-Cobb in Marietta, used to cook every night, but age and failing eyesight made her wish seem impossible. When employees of the nursing home found out about Birchfield's dream, they helped her make a berries-and-cream cake to serve to her fellow residents. "She hadn't baked a cake for 37 years," says Beville, who snapped photos of the cooking affair for Second Wind's newsletter. "Mom loves sweets," says Birchfield's daughter, Diane Hicks, who watched from the sidelines. "We had dessert every single night growing up."

Another Rhodes resident, Booker Linkhorn, was 75 when he realized a dream through Second Wind. A former pitcher for a farm team during the 1940s, before African Americans could play Major League Baseball, Linkhorn was in baseball heaven in 2003 when three nursing home employees took him to an Atlanta Braves game. "I hollered, 'Hey, Sheffield, hit one for me," Linkhorn recalls, his eyes reflecting the excitement of hobnobbing with outfielder Gary Sheffield, who played for the Braves at that time. "He did and yelled back, 'That one's for you, Booker.'" Now 79, Linkhorn still relishes the memories.

Funded primarily through donations, Second Wind Dreams grew so fast that Beville left behind her six-figure geriatrics consulting job in the late 1990s. With her banker husband's blessing, she volunteered 40 or more hours a week to the organization until she hired an executive director in 2006. She continues as CEO and still puts in countless hours.

"We have become much more active with youth groups in recent years," Beville says. "Our program now encompasses students of all ages who go into the elder care communities, discover dreams, and, along with their school or youth groups, start making them come true."

The results have been incredible. "Kids are really making connections that they never thought they would make, and elders are soaking up the youth that fills the place with laughter and action. The young people's 'can do' attitude becomes contagious," she says.

"We also have a Gifts of Light program where we adopt elders with no family support who will get nothing at holiday time," says Beville. "We find out who they are and what they would like, and our 'elves' adopt the elders, purchase their gift or gifts, and visit them one-on-one on Christmas Eve, Christmas Day, or any other holiday the resident holds dear. In 2006, we served more than 600 elders with approximately 400 volunteers in the metro Atlanta area. In 2007, we're rolling out the program nationwide."

Beville's selflessness has been acknowledged with numerous awards. Among the latest, she was named one of seven "women of worth" by cosmetics giant L'Oreal Paris in its inaugural award ceremony in 2006 to honor women who make a difference in their communities, adding beauty to the world through words and deeds. But Beville's greatest reward is the look on the face of each elderly person when a dream is fulfilled.

"I love my work so much," says Beville, who believes her special empathy for elders stems from the helplessness she felt when temporarily paralyzed by polio as a child. "I love to hold elders, to brush their hair. I'm so enamored with the aging process and the miracle of that and how we see aging and how families handle it."

Second Wind's mission also includes changing public perceptions of elders and the aging process. "For our society, aging is viewed as a negative thing," Beville says. "But when dreams come true for elders, we notice that the family gets to see their parents as they used to be, the elders are surprised that they are still able to do things they thought they couldn't, the caregivers are so proud of the elders, and the volunteers come away saying that they will never look at aging in such a negative way again. Each dream, then, is a gift to everyone's soul."

—Elaine Hobson Miller

Wisdom is yours when you honor your elders, listen to their thoughts and dreams, and celebrate the miracle of life together.

Editor's Note: Pollyanna Birchfield died shortly after baking her last cake, not an uncommon occurrence after an elderly person's dream has been fulfilled, according to Beville. "In some cases, we have found that having a dream come true gives the elder the release he or she needs to be able to feel a peace," she says.

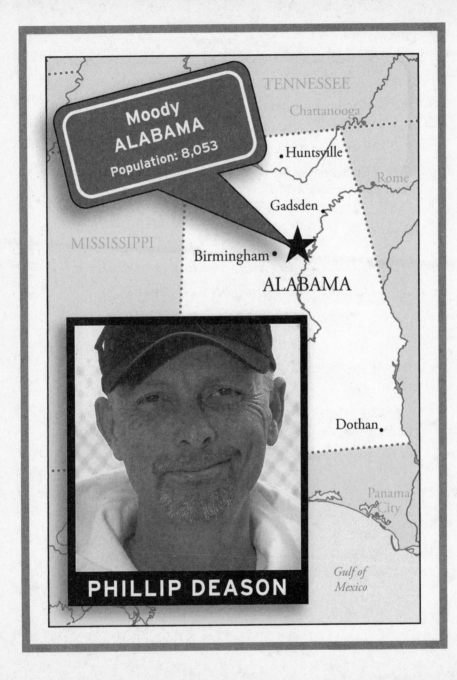

Moody
ALABAMA
Population: 8,053

TENNESSEE
Chattanooga
Huntsville
Rome
Gadsden
MISSISSIPPI
Birmingham
ALABAMA
Dothan
Panama City
Gulf of Mexico

PHILLIP DEASON

A League of Miracles

In 1996, Phillip Deason was approached by the mother of Corey Freeman, a spunky 3-year-old with Down syndrome who desperately wanted to play baseball. Deason, then president of the youth sports association in Moody, Alabama, put the youngster on a noncompetitive Cap Ball team, a precursor to tee-ball.

But after five years, Corey grew too big to play with the 3- and 4-year-olds, and Deason recognized the need for a baseball league for kids with special needs. In 2002, he created the Moody Miracle League, which now boasts more than 250 players.

"In regular youth associations, parents will holler because of a bad call or a child who didn't get to play," says Deason, 47, a city councilman in charge of Moody's parks and recreation department. "But at a Miracle League game, you hear them talk of wrenching decisions between buying a new automobile or their child an electric wheelchair. That puts it all into perspective."

Deason's search for a special needs team led him to the National Miracle League Association (NMLA), a Conyers, Georgia-based organization that formed after a Georgia coach started a special needs team in 1999. The NMLA priced a Miracle League field at about $400,000 in those days.

Fund-raising efforts for Moody's field began in 2002. Deason teamed with two Birmingham, Alabama, deejays, who collected $10,000 during a radio-thon. The city donated park space for the field, while Deason and other advocates blitzed local corporations for donations.

"We raised about $200,000 in funds, the rest in materials and manpower," Deason says.

The Moody Miracle League field was completed just in time for spring baseball season in 2003 and includes a flat, cushioned, synthetic playing surface with bases painted on to eliminate barriers for players with wheelchairs, walkers, or visual impairments. The league involves players from up to 10 Alabama counties that form 12 teams. Every player gets a chance to bat, every bat is a home run, and every game ends in a tie.

There are 159 Miracle League organizations nationwide, with 49 completed rubberized turf fields, 71 under construction and another 30 groundbreakings scheduled. In all, they serve approximately 25,000 children.

Moody's league has a regular spring season and an abbreviated fall season ending each year with a "Miracle Festival" at the park. Although the NMLA sets ages at 3 to 21, many Moody players are in their 20s and 30s, with two in their 70s. Some, like Corey Freeman, have Down syndrome, while others are autistic or suffer from cerebral palsy. One woman is blind, and her guide dog leads her around the bases.

Butch Hallmark, 19, is one of the "buddies" who walks bases with players or stands in the field alongside them to make sure they don't get hurt. "I've loved doing this since opening day," the University of Alabama sophomore says. "The player I buddy with can't talk, but he lets out this excited scream, so you know he enjoys it."

Playing baseball helps the participants feel good about themselves, says Patrick Shipp, who has umpired the games for several years. "Some can only blink or smile, but to see their faces light up when everyone stands and cheers for them, well, it's a blessing."

According to Corey's mom, Rhonda Freeman, the Miracle League field is a place where parents of children with special needs get to share their stories and where her son, now 14, gets a recreational outlet to let off steam and energy. "Corey has a blast there," she says.

So does Kamiko White, 15, the daughter of league director Rod White and his wife, Karen. Like many parents of special needs children, the Whites used to avoid ballparks because they knew that Kamiko, who has Down syndrome, could not play competitive ball. "Kamiko has been playing for the Moody Miracle League since its opening season in 2003, when she was 11," says her mom. "This has opened up more social activities for her, even beyond baseball, and she has made a lot of friends. In 2004, she was a cheerleader for the Moody Youth Association."

Deason, a modest man who prefers to stay in the background, credits donors and volunteers for the league's success. However, parents and volunteers call him "the heart and soul" of the league, convinced that his involvement has been crucial to its success.

"I don't feel like we'd be where we are now, debt-free, if not for Phillip," says Renae Harris, a volunteer who helped in the fund-raising efforts.

Deason says *he* has received the greatest reward from the Moody Miracle League. He recalls his teenage years when he picked on people who were different from him. "Now, I watch our two 70-year-old players and wonder how many years they wanted to play baseball and were made fun of by people like me," he says. "I've got to believe the majority of my volunteers have these same feelings."

—ELAINE HOBSON MILLER

With heart and determination, and the ability to see change, the seemingly impossible becomes within reach of us all.

Fresno

Ojai
CALIFORNIA
Population: 7,862

CALIFORNIA

Pacific Ocean

Lompoc

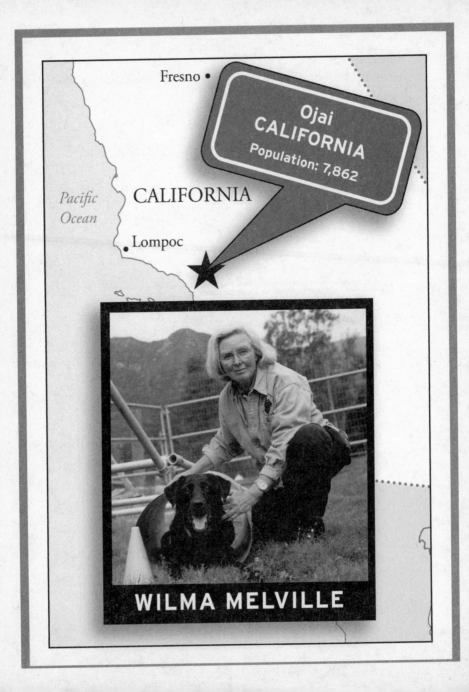

Training Rescue Teams

When Wilma Melville, of Ojai, California, retired as a physical education teacher in 1988, she created a "to do" list that included, "Learn to train a dog to do something significant."

"As a youngster I always had a dog, and I would train them to sit, stay and come," says Melville, 73. "But I wanted to do more."

So Melville began disaster search and rescue canine training, which involves a handler giving a dog signals to sniff out a live person trapped under rubble. However, after three years of training once a month with local handlers in southern California, Melville was not satisfied with her or her dog's progress. "I knew [the training] was being badly taught because I was a teacher," Melville says.

Determined, she began lessons with professional dog trainer Pluis Davern in Gilroy, California. Within a year and a half, she and her black Labrador, Murphy, passed the Federal Emergency Management Agency (FEMA) certification test for search and rescue dogs and joined a California-based disaster response team.

On April 9, 1995, FEMA deployed Melville and Murphy to Oklahoma City to aid in recovery efforts following the bombing of the Alfred P. Murrah Federal Building. They covered large areas of rubble, with Murphy barking loudly to indicate where victims were buried, thereby saving precious time for firefighters. Despite the satisfaction of helping in a national crisis, Melville was startled to see other task forces arriving without rescue dogs and to realize Murphy was one of only 15 FEMA-certified search and rescue dogs in the country. "If everybody is getting trained the way I had been trained originally," she recalls saying, "it's no wonder there are so few certified dogs."

Within months, Melville founded the National Disaster Search Dog Foundation to train more canine teams. In that first year, she used $44,000 of her own money to launch the initiative. By 1997, the foundation graduated its first class—three Sacramento, California, firefighters. "I had already decided that I needed to work with firefighters," she says. "They are the first on a scene of disaster, and they have the time to train."

Today, the foundation is funded through private donations and picks up the $10,000 tab for each student's training. Nearly all students are firefighters, and classes are grouped together based on geography.

Melville says three ingredients account for the foundation's 85 percent training success rate: the right dog, the right handler, and the right professional training for both. The foundation generally looks for dogs at animal shelters and sends the animals to Davern's training center in Gilroy for six months. The dogs are then paired with handlers, and their training as a team lasts one year.

In 2005, 16 teams of handlers and dogs graduated from the training program, and 23 teams graduated in 2006. Since its launch in 1996, the foundation has trained 53 FEMA-certified canine teams.

Mike Connors, a firefighter with the Coral Gables (Fla.) Rescue Department, and his dog, Hobbes, are one such team. In 2005, the duo put their training to good use. "We went to New Orleans for 28 days after Hurricane Katrina," says Connors, who completed the training in 2000. "Everything we'd trained for at Search Dog we ran across in New Orleans."

In 2006, Melville stepped down as the foundation's executive director, but she continues to help with fundraising and acts as Search Dog's spokeswoman.

"To me, Wilma is an amazing woman," says Debra Tosch, the organization's new executive director. "Few people would have had the perseverance to get through all of the obstacles she faced to get the foundation off the ground. Wilma took a vision and turned it into something that has made a difference in our country."

—Leah Ingram

When you see a need,
work one step at a time to help fill the void.

Paxico
KANSAS
Population: 211

St. Joseph

Topeka

Kansas City

Russell

Great Bend

KANSAS

STEVE HUND JR.

Restoring Stoves—and a Town

Steve Hund Jr. paid $15 for a rusty potbellied stove at an auction in 1971 to heat his drafty house. He and his wife, Kathryn, lived in a fixer-upper farmhouse and needed cheap heat. They were impressed by the efficiency of the stove he bought at the auction, as were friends.

Hund, who worked on the Rock Island Railroad at the time, soon was buying stoves and fixing them up for friends. As his stove collection grew, the then 24-year-old talked a reluctant banker into giving him a $2,500 loan to buy the vacant C. J. Glotzbach General Store in boarded-up downtown Paxico. He used the money to open Mill Creek Antiques in 1973.

Today, Hund restores about 100 stoves a year, including wood-burning cook stoves, and scrambles to keep up with demand from people reclaiming family heirlooms and seeking period furnishings for their Victorian-era homes. Reconditioned stoves sell for $3,000 to $20,000, depending on their rarity and ornamentation.

The thrill and challenge for Hund is transforming the rusty heirlooms that people haul in, often in boxes and missing parts, into beautifully restored stoves that warm hearts as well as homes.

"The stoves remind people of a simpler time," says Hund, now 59, surrounded by 40 gleaming cast-iron heating and cooking stoves at Mill Creek Antiques. "People remember going into Grandma's house and smelling apple pie baking in the woodstove."

More than practical sources of heat, the antique wood- and coal-burning stoves from the 1850s to 1920s are works of art embellished with floral designs and scenes and nickel-plated trim.

Hund also restores stoves for museums, including the 1859 Fort Larned military post in Larned, Kansas, and President Harry S. Truman's farmhouse in Grandview, Missouri.

Restoration involves disassembling the cast-iron stoves, sandblasting them to remove rust, locating or casting new pieces, and nickel-plating the trim for sentimental customers.

"I remember my granddad sitting in the old wicker rocker beside the stove and smoking his pipe," says Enid Crabb of Council Grove, Kansas, who paid Hund $930 to refurbish her great-grandparents' stove. "Granny would pop popcorn on the stove and put sugar on it." Her children are the fifth generation warmed by the stove. "I love the family continuity," she says.

As Hund's sales heated up, so did business in downtown Paxico. Other antique dealers were inspired to buy or lease buildings in the town, which looks more 1907 than 2007 with its brick streets and gingerbread-trimmed storefronts. Today, a dozen antique stores attract thousands of bargain hunters on weekends.

The town's centerpiece is Mill Creek Antiques, housed in an 1886 building with its original fixtures and counters, pressed-tin ceiling, and creaky wooden floors. Hund fixed up the basement in the sprawling half-block-long store so townspeople would have a place for musical performances and community get-togethers.

"Every little town I've ever seen has one person like Steve who has a vision and is relentless," says Mike Holper, owner of Old Woodman Antiques, who visited Hund three years ago to sell him some furniture and ended up leasing a building in Paxico.

Hund shrugs off praise, but acknowledges that Paxico has undergone a transformation since he began restoring stoves more than 35 years ago. "I looked down the street one day and it had happened. We didn't have any empty buildings."

Or any cold toes among customers and neighbors sitting around the crackling stoves in downtown Paxico—where Hund keeps the home fires burning.

—Marti Attoun

Reclaim and recycle whenever possible, appreciating the power of both our heritage from the past and our hope for the future.

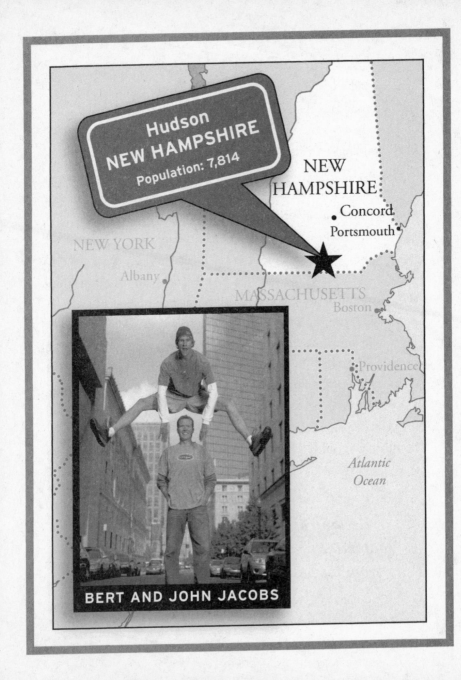

Hudson
NEW HAMPSHIRE
Population: 7,814

NEW HAMPSHIRE
Concord
Portsmouth
NEW YORK
Albany
MASSACHUSETTS
Boston
Providence
Atlantic Ocean

BERT AND JOHN JACOBS

Life Is Good

Do what you like. Like what you do.

It's a philosophy that brothers Bert and John Jacobs have embraced in life to become successful in business. The result of their down-to-earth, glass-half-full attitudes is a happy little brand called Life is good. And the success of the brand over the last 13 years says a lot about what Americans are hungry for: something positive.

Life is good, the ever-evolving lifestyle brand of happy-looking clothing and accessories that began as a two-man mobile T-shirt business, has evolved into a 250-person staff in Hudson, New Hampshire, and a 22-person design center on Boston's tony Newbury Street—just across from where police used to run the brothers off for peddling shirts without a legal permit.

Bert, 42, and John, 39, hail from the Boston suburb of Needham, Massachusetts and are the youngest of six children. Both college-educated brothers dabbled in substitute teaching to help subsidize their fledgling brand in the early days.

Enjoying life is one thing the brothers have never forsaken as their modest T-shirt, which they designed in 1989 and originally peddled out of the back of a van, has grown into an $80 million business with international reach. They acknowledge they've made mistakes along the way, but they never faltered from their original intent of impacting American culture more positively than any other brand in history. Only now, they've widened their scope to include the entire world.

"It hasn't been hard to stay focused," Bert says. "How can you preach this message and not live it? We've defined branding as knowing who we are and acting like it. We are such regular guys and we don't know how not to be regular guys."

The iconic face of Life is good is Jake, a happy little stick figure wearing a beret, cool shades, and an infectious smile who loves to hike, play Frisbee, drink coffee, and—you got it—enjoy life. He's a regular guy who doesn't know how not to be a regular guy.

Jake was among many drawings the brothers had been toying with as they searched for a potential brand to develop. "We had put the drawing of Jake on the wall [of our apartment], and one of our friends wrote next to it 'This guy's got life figured out,' and that resonated with us," says Bert.

Jake was an instant hit three days later when the brothers sold their new T-shirts at a local street fair. "Not only did we sell 48 shirts in 45 minutes, the first person who bought one was a Harley dude. The next one was a skateboard kid, then a 45-year-old schoolteacher. We saw completely different people buying the exact same shirt," Bert recalls.

In the years since, people everywhere have embraced Life is good, and the Jacobs think they know why.

"The media are tremendously focused on what's wrong with our world," Bert says. "Nobody has an opportunity to focus on what's right. You wouldn't think our clothing would be so different than what's out there, but it is. People are drawn to it."

It's clear that Bert, who handles business development, and John, who holds up the creative end, aren't stiff-shirt corporate types. As soon as the profit margin would allow, they established a charitable division to raise money for children's causes. Instead of stuffy black-tie gala fundraisers, they opted for something more fun. The company created two annual outdoor festivals that raise money for charities for children. During its annual pumpkin festival last October, the company recorded a world-record 30,128 pumpkins lit in one spot and raised more than a half million dollars for Camp Sunshine, a retreat center in Casco, Maine, for families of children with life-threatening illnesses. Its spring watermelon festival supports Project Joy in Brookline, Massachusetts, which helps children who have experienced trauma, including natural disaster, war, domestic violence, and abuse.

Steve Gross, founder of Project Joy and a longtime friend of the Jacobs's, says the Life is good brand captures the spirit of Bert and John. "Those guys have a really powerful energy," Gross says.

"They are fun. Both of those guys are so positive. When you hang out with them, you feel like you are a part of something. When you wear the clothes, you feel like you are a part of a movement to get as much out of life as you possibly can."

Bert says that although the business is thriving and expanding, it's what they can do with that profit that excites the brothers. That's why they decided early on never to sell the company, no matter how attractive the offer. He says being able to impact the lives of children is much more fulfilling than a pile of money and a Mercedes-Benz.

"If we sold it for a barrel of money, would it be satisfying enough?" asks Bert. "We both came to the conclusion that, no, being wealthy doesn't mean a lot to us now. Instead, we want to harness the brand to make a true impact on our culture."

Being a good corporate citizen is one way to do that. "If we can be a business for profit and turn that profit into helping people, that's what has us revved up right now," Bert says.

—Melonee McKinney Hurt

Success is about more than money in the bank.

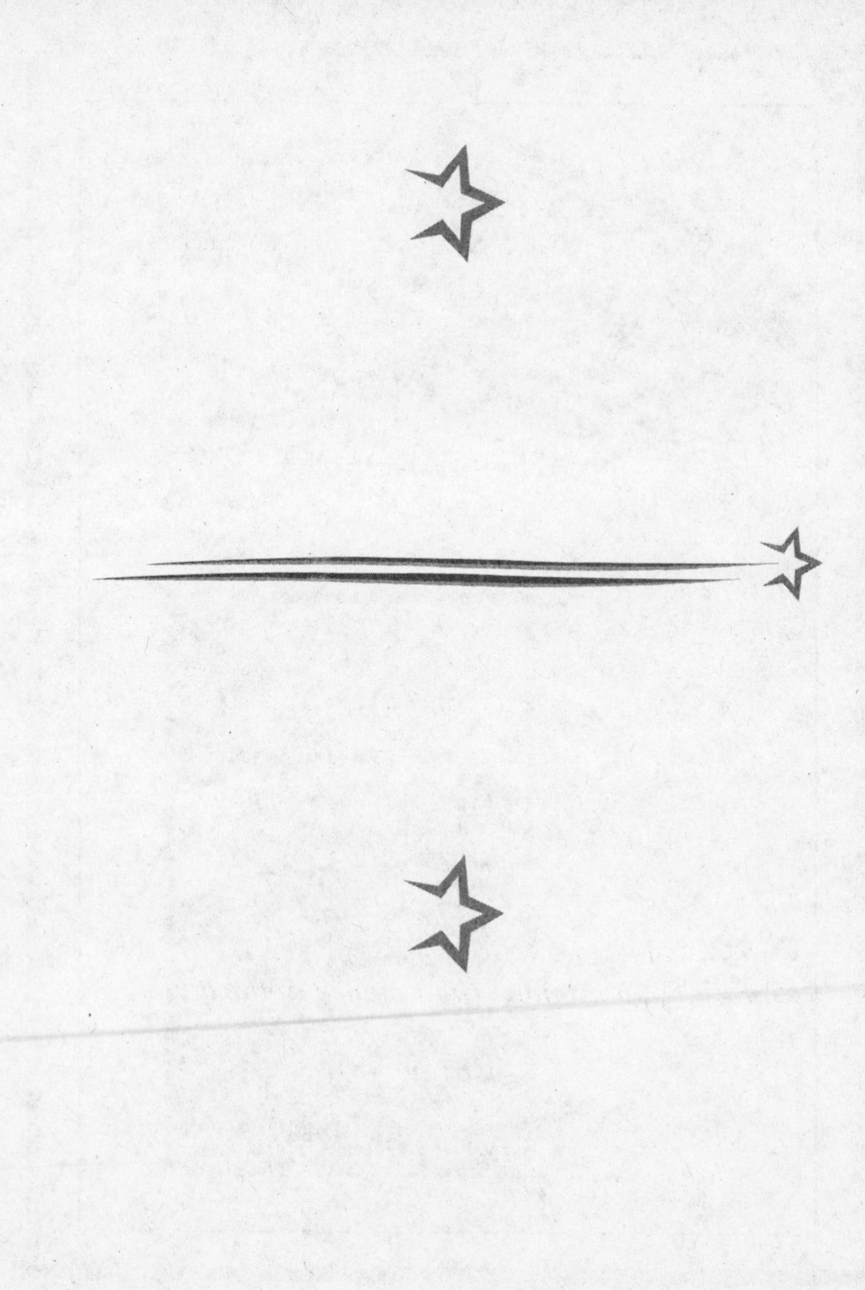

Roanoke
Norfolk
Belhaven
NORTH CAROLINA
Population: 1,968
NORTH CAROLINA
Charlotte
Fayetteville
Columbia
SOUTH
CAROLINA
Hilton
Head
Island
Atlantic
Ocean
DR. CHARLES BOYETTE

Good Doctor, Good Deeds

In September 2003, when Hurricane Isabel brought ferocious winds and a 6-foot water surge into the coastal town of Belhaven, North Carolina, the local hospital was forced to shut its doors. In response, Dr. Charles Boyette turned his home into a makeshift emergency room, treating anyone who needed help.

One such resident was Michi Smith, then 70, who was injured during the hurricane. "He's always there when I need him," says Smith, a longtime patient of Boyette.

In his 40 years as a selfless caregiver in Belhaven, Boyette has gone the extra mile on many occasions, including the time he removed himself from traction—with a ruptured disk—to deliver a baby and tend to a heart attack patient.

"He's just a good doctor and a good person and always puts the patients first," says Elizabeth Wilkins, who has been Boyette's office manager for 35 years. Wilkins recalls how the doctor went out of his way to tend to her arthritic mother and regularly dropped by their house to check on her.

Wilkins also remembers how the "good doctor" pays utility bills and makes funeral arrangements for those who can't afford them; buys clothes for poor patients; sought out a new cat for a bereaved patient whose feline was run over by a car; and outfitted the Belhaven High School football team with uniforms when funds were scarce. Boyette says helping residents in need is all part of the job, and he prefers to do it "without fanfare."

The 71-year-old doctor's good deeds are far-reaching and applauded. They collectively sealed his designation as Country Doctor of the Year for 2003 by Staff Care, a temporary-physician firm based in Irving, Texas. He more than met the requirements—a physician in a town smaller than 25,000 who goes far and above the normal routine of a doctor. The award caps a long list of accolades, including 1978 North Carolina Physician of the Year, 1988 Belhaven Jaycees Outstanding Public Servant of the Year, and the University of North Carolina School of Medicine's Distinguished Service Award in 1996.

Boyette was born in 1935 and grew up in Chadbourn, North Carolina, where he deplored the fact that the town didn't have a doctor and "we had to take Dad, who had diabetes, and other family members several miles for help." That struggle made a lasting impression and set him on a path toward medicine. He earned his bachelor's degree in history at the University of North Carolina at Chapel Hill and then went on to earn a medical degree at UNC's School of Medicine.

In 1964, after serving four years in the Navy, he was discharged and immediately headed for Belhaven after a friend implored him to settle there. At the time, the town had just one aging doctor, so Boyette set up a viable medical practice, which today serves about 100 patients daily and boasts a medical staff of five. In addition to his work at Boyette Medical Clinic, he makes regular rounds at an area hospital, nursing home, and healthcare facility.

Although providing quality, comprehensive medical care is his primary goal, Boyette has looked after Belhaven's municipal health as well, serving as mayor for nearly 30 years until 2005 and now holding a seat on the town council. "I have always had an avid interest in community affairs and feel a responsibility to be involved," Boyette says. "My mayoral duties actually complement my responsibilities as a doctor."

Boyette has spurred layers of improvements that have revitalized the town. Besides saving Belhaven's hospital from bankruptcy, he has relentlessly sought funds for daycare centers, recreational facilities, a library, expanding the water treatment plant, scholarships for community college students, and the elevation of 383 homes prone to flooding.

His energy, dedication, and compassion have elicited praises echoed by Tim Johnson, Belhaven's town manager since 1984.

"He's the ultimate professional and businessman and not one to rest on his laurels," Johnson says. "He works 85 hours a week, he's never on vacation, and he always tries to make things better. Belhaven is mighty lucky to have him."

—Ann Goebel

Do what you can, while you can,
as long as you can.

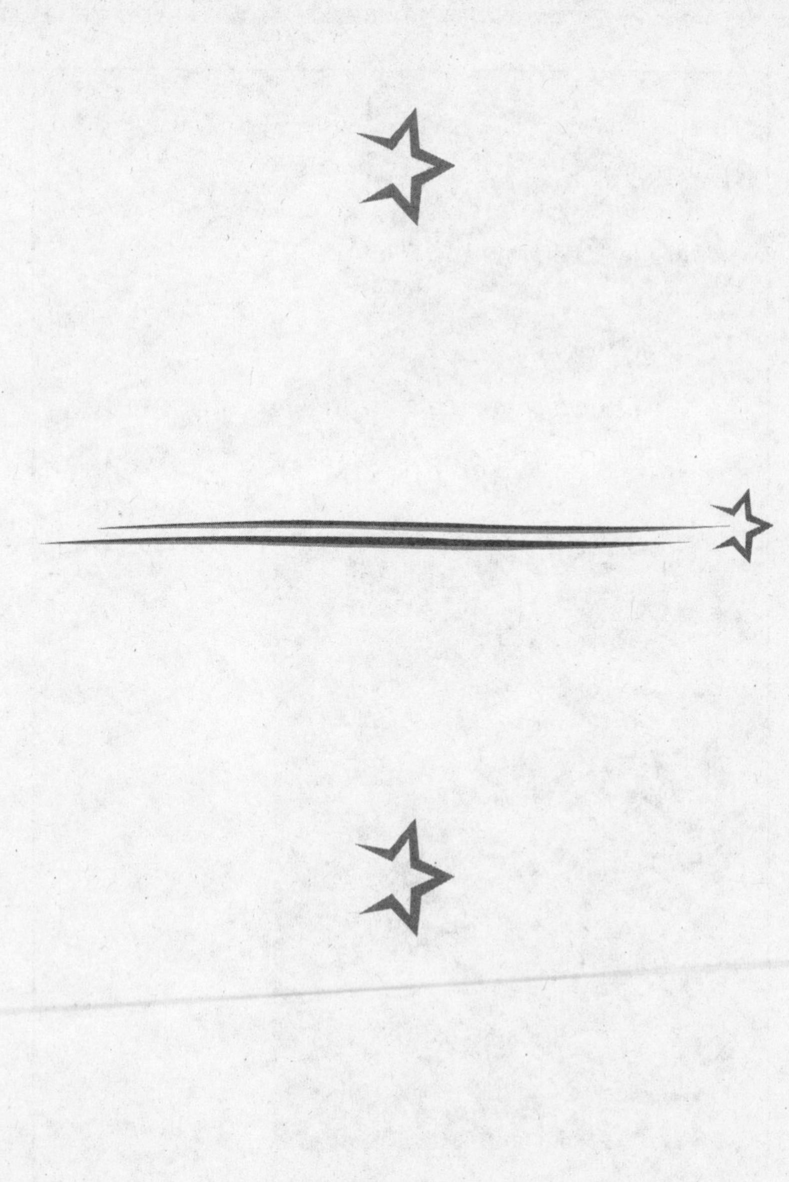

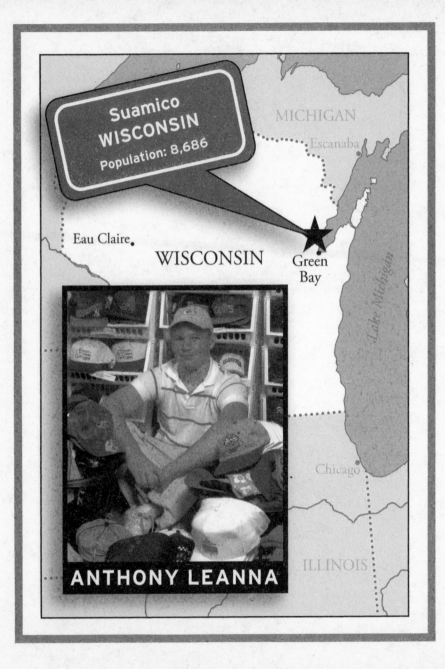

Suamico
WISCONSIN
Population: 8,686

MICHIGAN

Escanaba

Eau Claire

WISCONSIN

Green Bay

Lake Michigan

Chicago

ILLINOIS

Distributing Heavenly Hats

Anthony Leanna, of Suamico, Wisconsin, was only 8 years old when he first visited his ailing grandmother in the hospital. "I really loved my grandma, and I was afraid she'd die," says Anthony, whose grandmother, Darlene Chartier, had undergone surgery for breast cancer in 1999. "I was also afraid she'd lose her hair like the other cancer patients I saw in the hospital."

Although his grandmother didn't lose her hair—she had radiation treatment rather than chemotherapy—Anthony couldn't forget about all of the patients who did, especially the kids. "I decided I was going to collect hats for cancer patients to cheer them up," he says.

At age 10, Anthony started on a small scale in the spring of 2001. With a little help from his parents, he set out two plastic buckets to collect hats in front of stores in Suamico. "We were right behind him all the way," says mom Dee. "We thought it was great that he wanted to use his own time and energy to do this wonderful thing for others."

"After a couple of weeks, the buckets were full," recalls Anthony, now 15 and a sophomore at Bay Port High School in Green Bay, Wisconsin. "Then I contacted the hospital my grandma had been in, and others as well, and asked if they could use these brand new hats for cancer patients."

The response was so enthusiastic that Anthony kept his bucket collection going and looked for ways to expand his efforts. "I wanted to collect and distribute hats to people across the United States," he says. His solution was to form the nonprofit Heavenly Hats Foundation and set up a Web site to allow online visitors a place to offer donations or request hats.

One such visitor was Julie Wheeler, a preschool teacher in San Carlos, California, who underwent treatment in 2005 for breast cancer and lost all her hair. Wheeler was thrilled when a box of five hats—all in pink, as she had requested—arrived at her house less than a week later.

"I felt very loved and cared for by someone I don't even know," says Wheeler, who is cancer-free now. "Anthony even sent a sleeping cap to keep my head warm at night. He's an angel who touches so many lives."

One grateful mother wrote Anthony that the hats made all the difference when her 5-year-old son woke up crying over clumps of hair he found in his bed one morning. After explaining that "special medicine" to treat the "cancer boo-boo in his tummy" was making his hair fall out, she showed her son the hats that a teenage boy had sent him "so he would look cool just like a big kid."

He stopped crying, smiled, and tried on every hat. "You will never know how you touch the hearts of so many!!" the mom wrote.

Thanks to donations from individuals and hat companies, Heavenly Hats has distributed more than 102,000 hats to cancer patients in 275 hospitals across the nation.

Anthony's mother has long since left her job as an insurance agent to volunteer with the foundation, where she and her son put in 60 to 70 hours a week. "It's a real commitment," says Dee. "We sort through every hat donated, seal them in plastic bags and pack the boxes for shipping."

With the help of five to 10 volunteers, Anthony and his mother ship more than 3,000 hats a month from an 800-square-foot facility donated by a local company. Despite the high volume, the Leannas try to meet every special request, like a letter from a mother who wrote: "My little girl has lost her hair, and she could use a sun hat so she can go outside this summer." Of course, they provided her with summertime hats.

Anthony says that seeing all of the requests are what drives him to keep working. "Cancer patients need these hats, and we get hundreds of letters, calls, and e-mails from people saying thanks and how much it means to them," says Anthony, who also plays football and guitar and wants to be a television producer one day.

His grandmother has been cancer-free for more than five years now and is proud of Anthony's selflessness. "We keep scrapbooks on him and Heavenly Hats," says Mrs. Chartier.

Anthony's foundation has brought him a lot of public attention, such as appearances on the *Today Show* and *Good Morning America*, plus numerous awards. "He's very humble about it all," his father, Glen, says. "He doesn't really like the attention, but he does it for the benefit of Heavenly Hats. We're really proud of him and what he's doing."

—Kathleen Conroy

A simple, caring gesture can give someone the courage to face another day.

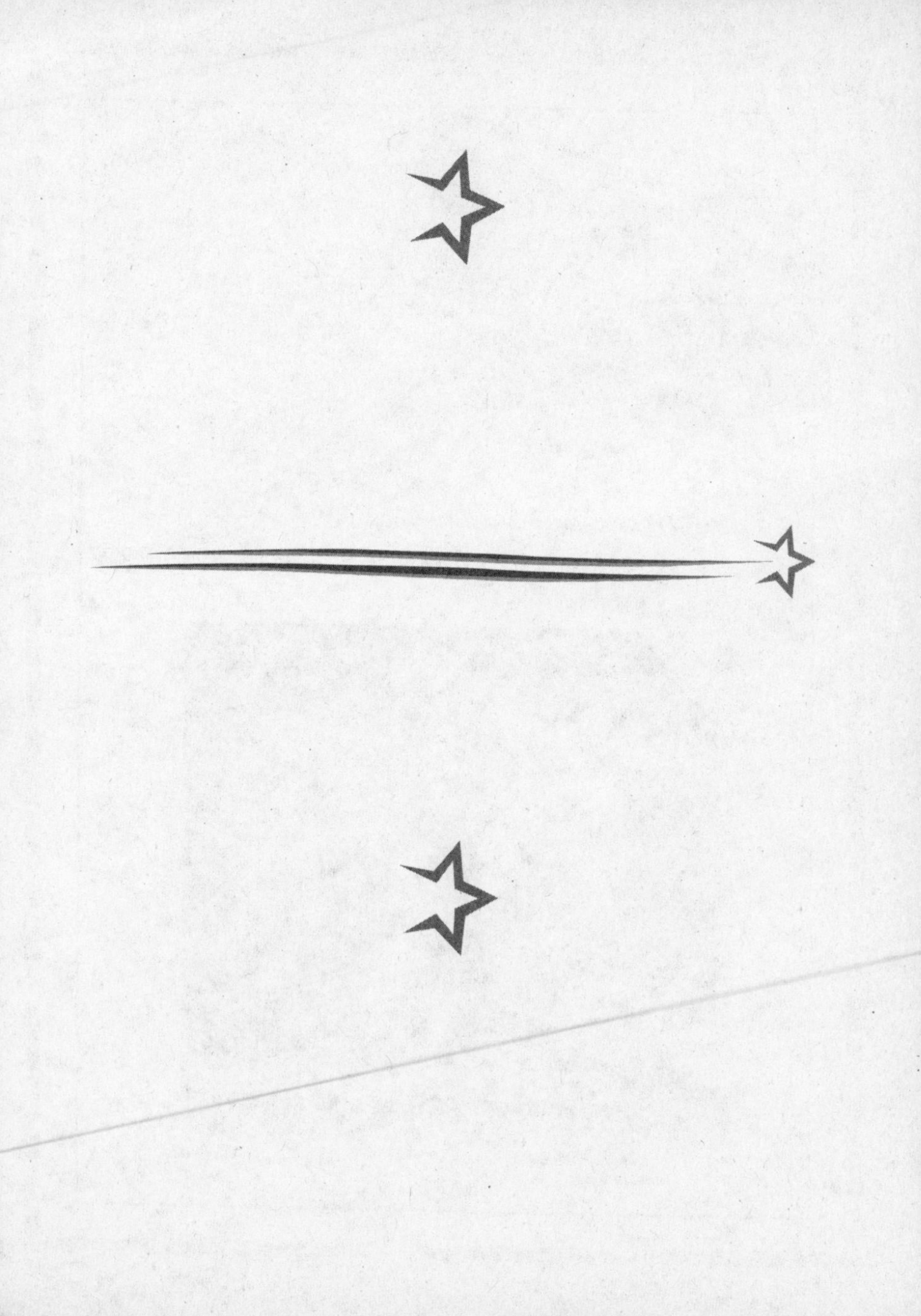

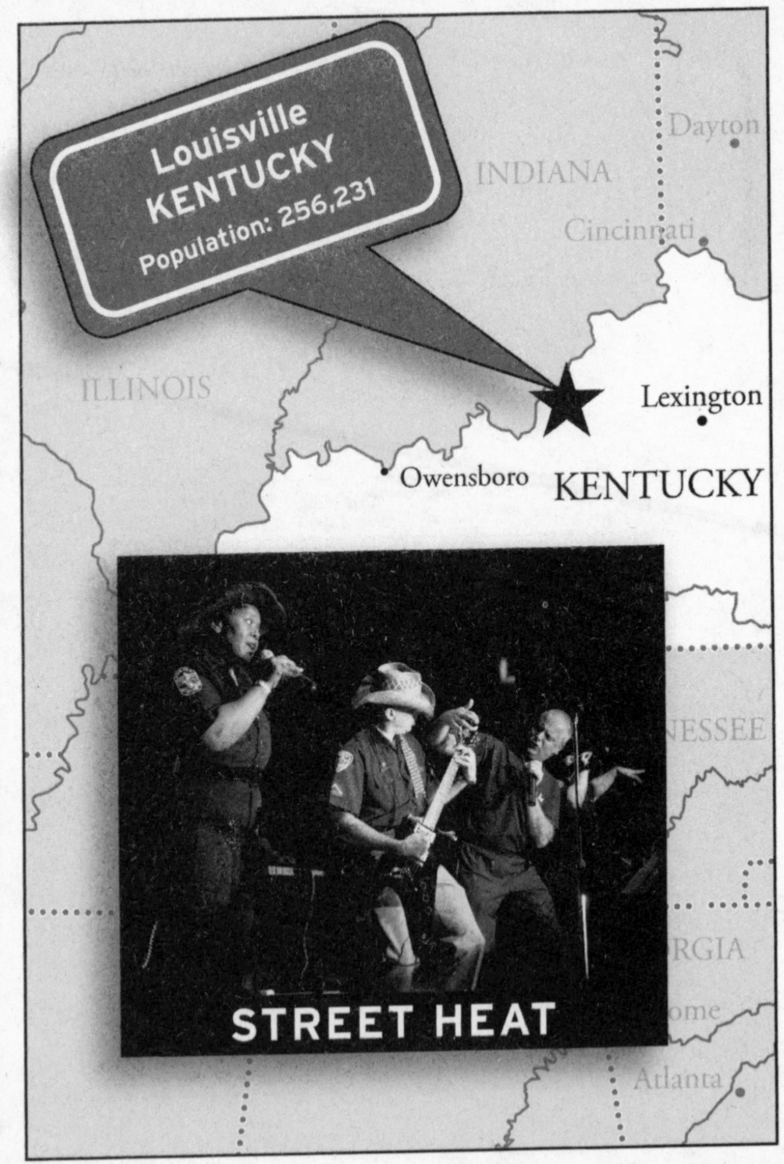
Louisville
KENTUCKY
Population: 256,231
Dayton
INDIANA
Cincinnati
ILLINOIS
Lexington
Owensboro
KENTUCKY
STREET HEAT
Atlanta

Rockin' Role Models

Seventh- and eighth-graders pour into the gym at South Laurel Middle School in London, Kentucky, quickly filling the bleachers. Doubly excited, they are not only excused from class, but it's for a rock 'n' roll concert.

As the last students settle into their seats, the band Street Heat launches into "Nod Your Head," a popular song from the movie *Men in Black II*, and the students rise to their feet to clap, sing along, and move to the groove.

Street Heat, based in Louisville, Kentucky, has been performing shows like this for 15 years at schools and other venues across Kentucky. But they're not your typical rock band. Its members are full-time police officers, sheriff's deputies, correctional officers, and firefighters who volunteer their time to use music to reach kids with messages about resisting drugs, avoiding violence, dealing with peer pressure, and believing in themselves.

Lead singer Billie Monk, 52, a correctional officer, says the reaction to the shows, especially in rural areas, is amazing. "We have actually gone to schools that have never seen a concert," she says. "Not a rock 'n' roll concert, anyway. You'd think we were Van Halen."

Police officer Sonya Talbott, 40, is a vocalist in the band. "Music crosses all boundaries," she says. "This is a positive connection with law enforcement where they can hear from someone other than their parents, other than their teachers, people who are encouraging them to do the right thing."

Street Heat works to stay current on music popular with kids. Their set list includes songs on the current pop charts, some rap, a bit of country, and even a few golden oldies. But they're careful to select songs with positive messages consistent with their musical mission. For example, "I'm a Believer," the old Monkees smash reworked for the movie *Shrek*, is presented with a commentary encouraging kids to "believe in themselves." Before singing the Maroon 5 hit "Harder to Breathe," Talbott tells the kids that making bad decisions can make you feel trapped, making it indeed "harder to breathe."

The group modifies the lyrics of some songs. The 1984 hit "Ghostbusters" becomes "Drugbusters." The tag line of the 1995 TLC pop hit "Waterfalls" ("Don't go chasing waterfalls") becomes "Don't go chasing drugs." Percussionist Barry Shaw, 46, a correctional officer, says the band hopes when kids hear the original tunes on their radios or iPods after a Street Heat show, they'll remember the Street Heat versions. Maybe, he says, "it will make them think about the anti-drug message we put out."

One of the most effective ways to measure the band's success is through the feedback after a performance—sometimes *years* after. It's not uncommon for the group to hear from former students, now adults, who say hearing Street Heat had a positive impact on their lives. "I don't remember much of my middle school years," says Montez Davis of Louisville, who saw Street Heat in the early 1990s. "But I remember Street Heat. Hearing how to be responsible, how not to get caught up in peer pressure, to respect your elders, to stay in school, and to just be a good person—it stuck with me."

The message also seems to be sticking with kids like South Laurel seventh-grader Kyle Smith. "I liked the music," says Smith, "and the whole point of it was good, too—don't do drugs."

Brooke Butler, an eighth-grader at Louisville's Farnsley Middle School, says Street Heat's music encourages kids not to follow the crowd. "You should just say no to drugs and drinking and smoking, instead of trying to fit in with other people," Butler says. "Let them try to fit in with you."

Firefighter and bass guitarist Gerald Shively, 43, says the members of Street Heat believe they're indeed making a difference, which is why the group has stayed together for so long.

"You hope that what we're doing does have an impact," he says. "That's why we put our hearts into it."

—Pam Windsor

Music can build bridges between people—and generations.

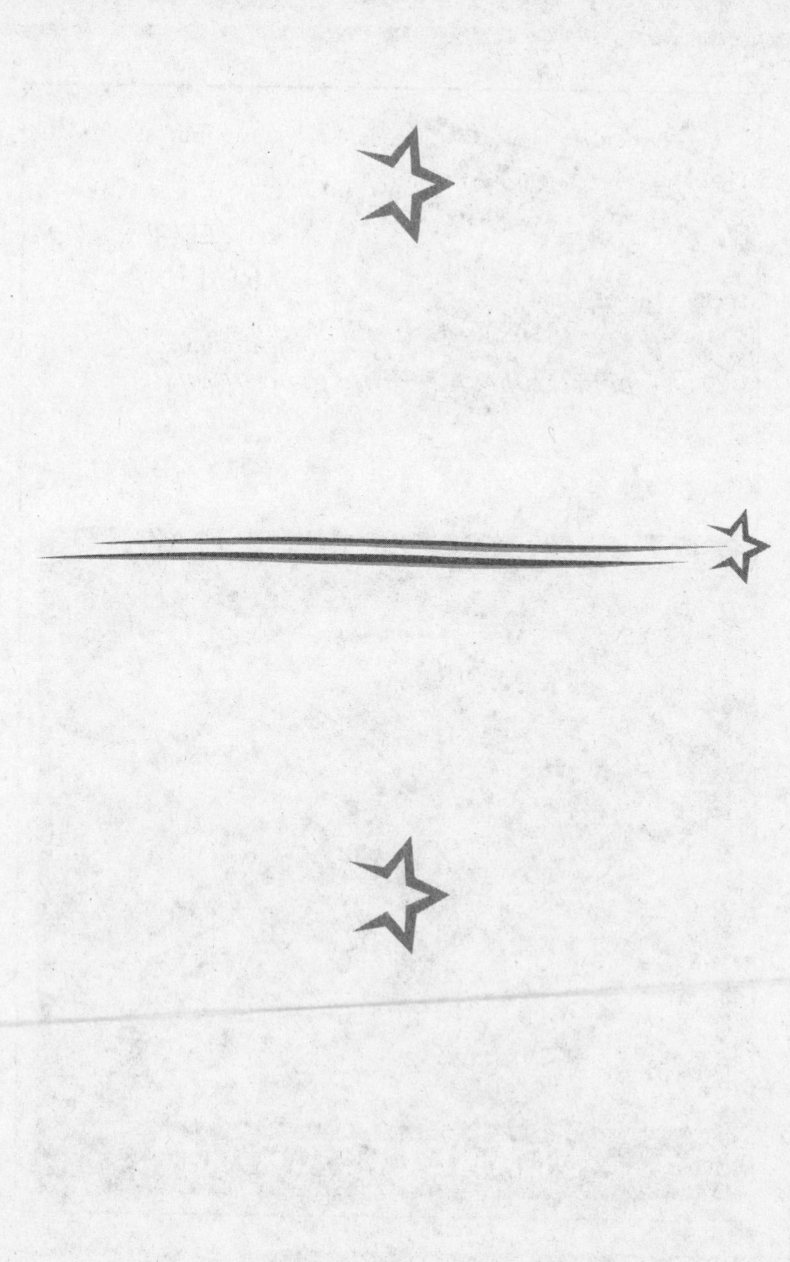

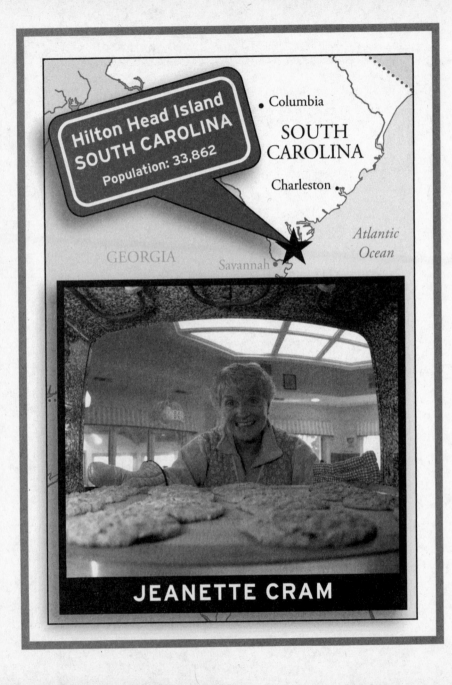

Hilton Head Island
SOUTH CAROLINA
Population: 33,862

Columbia

SOUTH CAROLINA

Charleston

Atlantic Ocean

GEORGIA

Savannah

JEANETTE CRAM

Treating the Troops

Two heavy-duty mixers rest on Jeanette Cram's kitchen countertop in Hilton Head Island, South Carolina, waiting to prepare dozens of chocolate chip, oatmeal raisin, or snickerdoodle cookies. Thanks to Cram's baking prowess, American soldiers in Middle Eastern war zones have been enjoying a sweet taste of home for more than 15 years.

"I think of it as a calling," Cram says.

When the Gulf War began in 1990, Cram started baking, packing, and shipping cookies to U.S. troops overseas. Her efforts began after she saw then president George H. W. Bush on television reading a soldier's letter asking for homemade treats. Cram turned to her husband, Jack, and said, "I can do that."

Since then, the 65-year-old grandmother's cookie count has risen faster than dough in a desert oven. "Once the press got hold of it, it just got bigger and bigger," says Cram, known far and wide as simply "The Cookie Lady." She estimates she and her assistants have sent nearly 200,000 cookies in the past 16 years and notes that her e-mail box stays filled with requests, sometimes 300 a month.

"It's amazing how just a little cookie can help their morale," she says of the soldiers who relish her treats—and the warm thoughts behind them.

Cram has about 40 "crumbs," as she calls them—volunteer assistants who help bake, pack, and ship.

Debbie Hudson saw her on *The Martha Stewart Show* last year and enlisted help from friends at the First Baptist Church in Cumming, Georgia. They immediately shipped 10,000 cookies to names on Cram's waiting list. "What Jeanette has done with her stamina and fortitude has been a miracle to watch unfold," Hudson says.

Are her recipes secret? "No, I'm a mama cooker, not a gourmet cooker," Cram says. "I use the chocolate chip cookie recipe from the back of the chocolate chip bag, the recipe from the oatmeal box for the oatmeal raisin cookies, and I found the snickerdoodle recipe on the Internet."

Shipping days in Cram's kitchen are a flurry of activity as she and several local "crumbs" pack the cookies—a dozen in each Baggie, five Baggies in each box. Cram uses shredded paper from her local sherriff's office, where she volunteers, for packing "when there's not enough bubble wrap," she says. Then, with a car full of cookies, Cram drives to the back door of the nearby post office and drops off packages that begin their 7 to 10-day journey to eager troops.

Janna Rowe of Victoria, Texas, says her husband, Army National Guard Maj. John Douglas Rowe, was one of Cram's lucky recipients. "She is a reminder that alongside our hero soldiers and their families, there are other heroes like Jeanette," Rowe says.

Cram talks excitedly about her 2005 visit to the Oval Office, where President George W. Bush presented her with a box bearing the presidential seal and filled with red, white, and blue M&Ms—an appropriate gift since her chocolate chip cookies are made with the hard-coated candies during the summertime, when chocolate chips tend to melt in transit.

Spending about four hours every day working on her cookie cause, Cram relies on donations to pay her overhead of about $800 a month. She recently obtained tax-deductible status from the Internal Revenue Service, which she hopes will lessen her expenses.

Cram shows off her double oven and her mixers, wishing for a professional mixer some day so she can make more dough at one time. KitchenAide donated one mixer—a refurbished model painted bright pink in honor of breast cancer awareness—to the two-time survivor of the disease. But whether she uses an industrial mixer or a hand mixer, it is the soldier recipients that she focuses on day after day.

How long will Cram keep the treats coming? "I'll quit when the wars quit," she says.

—Sandy Summers

Never underestimate how much even the simplest gestures can help.

Fresno

Lompoc
CALIFORNIA
Population: 41,103

Pacific
Ocean

CALIFORNIA

Santa Barbara

PHIL YEH

From Cartoons to the Classics

In 1986, Phil Yeh, a young cartoonist in Lompoc, California, set out in a borrowed van with a few like-minded friends on a sneaky mission: to entice kids to read by first hooking them with cartoons.

Troubled by the fact that so many Americans were functionally illiterate, he organized a group called Cartoonists Across America to encourage kids to dive into books. Beginning with a cross-country tour to 34 states and two Canadian provinces, Yeh (pronounced, "Yay") and his cohorts appeared at schools, shopping malls, and other public spots to paint murals, enlist literacy tutors, and give away original comic books with a reading-is-fun theme.

"We thought if the books had cartoons in them we could 'trick' people into reading," Yeh says with a smile. His comics featured colorful, kid-friendly characters, such as dinosaurs, who urged children with a catchy, do-or-die motto: "Read: Avoid Extinction."

Yeh knew his technique could succeed because it worked for him as a youngster growing up in New Jersey. "I'm dyslexic," says Yeh. "I was always a terrible speller. But pictures and cartoons helped me learn to read. People—both kids and adults—can learn when something visual is there."

The first tour was received well and built momentum for subsequent excursions. As word spread, famous cartoonists such as Charles "Snoopy" Schulz and Matt "The Simpsons" Groenig got on board, lending their endorsements or participating in Cartoonists Across America events. Barbara Bush, wife of then president George H. W. Bush, invited Yeh and his team to a reception at the Library of Congress in 1989, and corporations, including McDonald's, Chevron, and American Airlines, helped with funding.

Now 52, Yeh has been spreading the message for more than two decades with the help of his fellow cartoonists. They've signed up hundreds of reading tutors nationwide, given away thousands of comic books, and painted more than 1,500 public murals (and a few billboards and city buses) touting the benefits of reading. While about 15 U.S. artists are Yeh's chief collaborators, many more have contributed to bigger events, such as a 1990 mural painting in Budapest, Hungary, that attracted more than 100 cartoonists from 40 countries.

"Phil was definitely an inspiration to me," says Jon J. Murakami, a cartoonist for the *Hawaii Herald* newspaper who joined Yeh early in his campaign and has remained active in his stable of volunteers.

"His energy amazed me to no end. And he's still out there, trying to promote literacy and better the world."

Klaus Leven was a young artist in Recklinghausen, Germany, when he read about Yeh's work in 1995. He traveled to the United States just to meet Yeh and join the campaign. "Phil changed my life completely," says Leven, who says Yeh inspired him to create his own line of literate comics featuring characters Joey and Gonz. "I loved all the great things he was doing for kids and wanted to do that, too."

A 20th anniversary tour, organized around a five-month exhibition of Yeh's trademark dinosaur paintings, kicked off in April 2006 at the Cleveland (Ohio) Museum of Natural History. Yeh and friends went on to paint more than a dozen new murals across the country including the 20-foot masterpiece they splashed across the side of a truck in San Bernadino, California, in July with a little help from Phil Ortiz, another "Simpsons" cartoonist, and George Gladir, creator of Archie Comics' "Sabrina, the Teenage Witch."

The anniversary tour also spawned a new vehicle for reaching children: cartoon workshops. Yeh began appearing at schools and libraries to conduct hands-on training to teach children how to create their own comics. By the end of 2006, he had worked with some 600 aspiring cartoonists during more than 50 workshops nationwide.

"Our kids spend more time on video games and electronic entertainment than any other kids in the world," Yeh says. "If we can get them interested in reading, writing, and drawing their own stories, which is the goal of these workshops, then there is hope."

The efforts are working, according to George Munoz, 16, of Tustin, California. "Phil inspired me to read more, despite my dyslexia," says Munoz, who attended one of Yeh's workshops and now writes and draws his own comic books. "He made me understand how important [reading] is, if I'm going to become an artist like him some day."

Even though America's illiteracy rate is still a staggering statistic, Yeh's motivation is as powerful as ever, stoked by the positive feedback he hears from kids like Munoz.

"These workshops taught me that kids love to learn," says Yeh. "The American spirit is still alive in terms of kids wanting to be an artist or a writer. They just need someone to show them how."

—M. B. Roberts

Life presents each of us with obstacles and gifts. The blessing comes when the gift helps you overcome the obstacle, and you can help others in similar struggles, too.

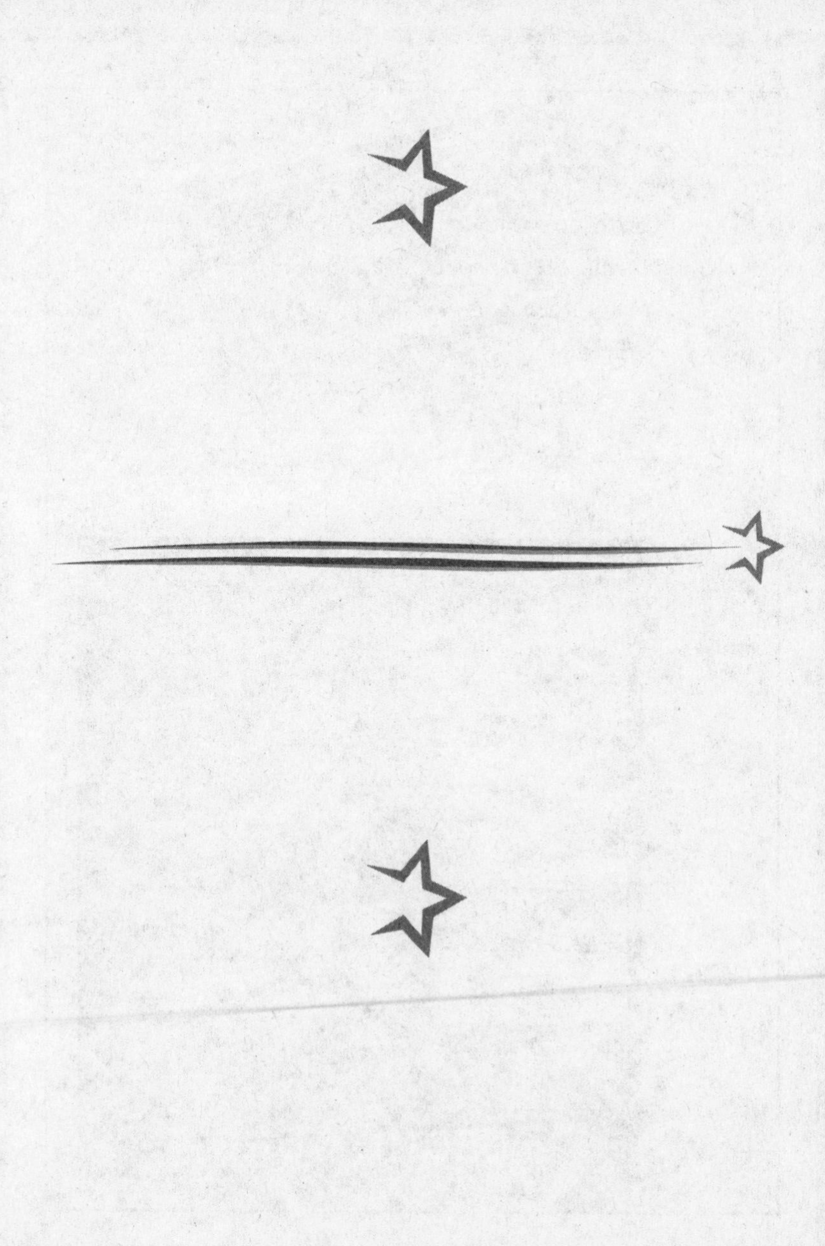

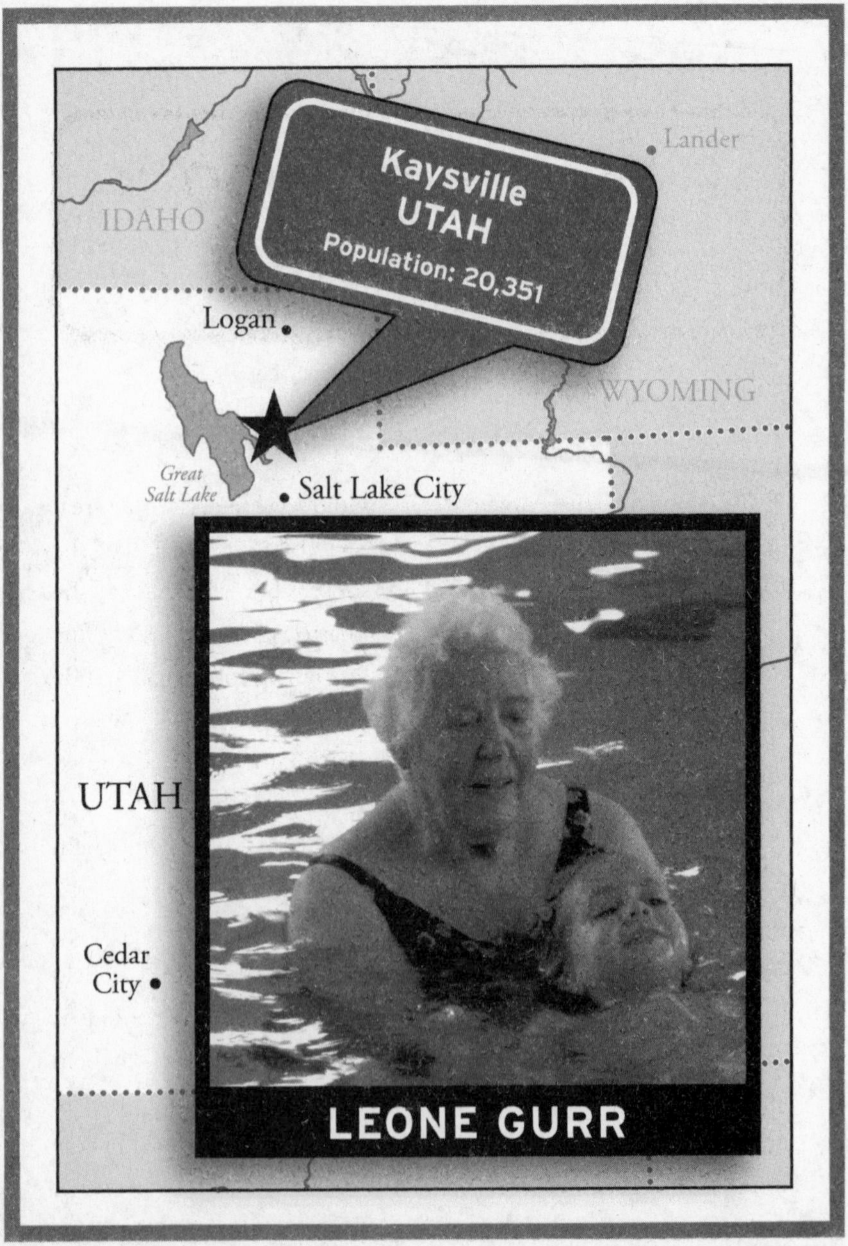

Kaysville
UTAH
Population: 20,351

Lander

IDAHO

Logan

WYOMING

Great Salt Lake

Salt Lake City

UTAH

Cedar City

LEONE GURR

Teaching 10,000 Swimmers

Despite the hardships that came with growing up in the Great Depression, Leone Gurr loved swimming so much that she found money to pay for years of lessons. When she was 16, she began teaching swimming—a love that has continued even as Gurr is well into her 70s. In all, she figures she's taught more than 10,000 people how to swim.

Gurr, of Kaysville, Utah, is convinced that every child should learn to swim—so convinced, in fact, that she introduced her four daughters and three sons to water as soon as she brought them home from the hospital. During their first baths, she let a little water trickle over their faces, and the babies naturally held their breath. Then she increased the water, little by little, until they held their breath whenever their faces were immersed. This technique is similar to how she gently coaches her students—most of them children—to dip their faces into her backyard pool. When they're comfortable with that, they're on their way to swimming and ready to learn emergency recovery skills.

"In a recovery, you put your arms down, bring your knees up to your chest and raise your head," says Gurr, 78. The difference between drowning and being able to keep your head above water is as simple as that. In addition to this personal water safety essential, she taught all her students basic lifesaving skills.

"I tell them to look around and see what's available to extend to the person in the water who's in trouble so that they can pull them in—a pole, clothing, a stick, a towel. We want to be sure that children keep something between them and the victim, so we don't have a double drowning."

The most challenging thing about Gurr's 60 years as a swimming instructor is that the demand for her classes grew and grew. To keep them small enough so children could learn swimming properly and safely, she began charging a small fee, but donated the money to a charity of the students' choice.

Gurr has difficulty walking now and doesn't have the stamina to teach as many classes as she used to, but she rests easier knowing that some of her students are teaching others to swim.

Matthew Cullimore put his water skills to professional use. He started giving swimming lessons at age 12 and, during high school, worked as a lifeguard at a local camping resort, saving enough money to go on a two-year mission to Portugal for his church. Then by working as a pool manager, he put himself through college and graduated from the University of Utah in 2002, thanks in part to the confidence he gained from Gurr's instruction.

"I remember the way she taught," he says. "She never really made me feel like she was critiquing what I was doing. She had such a sweet way about her. She really let you know she cared about you."

Another student, Nancy Lessmann, had some frightening experiences in the water as a child and was terrified even of getting near it. But at age 52, she joined Gurr's children's beginner class. Today, she's a confident swimmer and, to celebrate, even had a pool installed in her own backyard.

"Leone helped me to not be afraid of the water," Lessmann says, "and I finally jumped off the diving board into eight feet of water. I did it because I trusted that if I didn't come back up, she'd come get me."

—Laurel Holliday

If you really want to touch lives, be a teacher.

Editor's Note: One year after *American Profile* published this story in 2003, Leone Gurr died of cancer at age 79. Gurr is buried in Kaysville and leaves behind literally thousands of people who now know how to swim because of her patience, instruction, and encouragement.

Elk City
OKLAHOMA
Population: 10,510

KANSAS

OKLAHOMA

Oklahoma City

Amarillo

Lawton

Decatur

TEXAS

Waco

Temple

Cowboy for Hire

Among that rare breed known as cowboy, Vaughn Kennemer is rarer still. He's a full-time, freelance cowboy who hires himself out for day work to ranchers in the rolling red hills, wooded river bottoms, and mesquite canyons of his native Oklahoma.

Kennemer has earned a reputation for roping the mean ones—errant cows determined to get away and big bulls nobody else can catch.

"When the bull has nothing on his mind but to kill you and your horse and he has the weapons on the top of his head to do it with, it gets interesting," says Kennemer, 43. "When you pull tight on a 2,200-pound bull for the first time and he stands up on both hind legs and goes to walking off with your horse, you wonder about your intelligence. As bad as it may seem when the bull is yanking your horse around, it gets a lot worse when he goes the other way and comes up the rope."

Many who hire this modern-day cowpoke are small ranchers with other jobs who lack the time to handle branding, vaccinating, worming, or ear tagging their own cattle. Even some large ranches with regular crews need extra help when penning cattle or handling big jobs like branding. In the fall and spring, Kennemer is hired to do pregnancy tests on cows.

His base of operations is his own ranch in Elk City, Oklahoma. Other ranchers often take cows to him, since it's cheaper than having Kennemer set up his portable wheel pens and chute in the ranchers' own pastures. He treats sick cows or catches a cow that has wire around her leg, a common occurrence when wire or bailing twine gets left in the pasture. He also pulls a few calves during calving season.

Although he has never been seriously hurt while plying his cowboy trade, he has had horses gored—once by a bull and once by a cow. The horses recovered, and are much wiser for the experience.

"I don't get called to catch something unless most other options have been exhausted, therefore the animals I catch are typically mean, mad, and know every trick in the book," Kennemer says.

He's had his share of bruises and stitches, but contends that "cowboying" is no rougher on the body than any other type of hard work. "I'm not on a cane or crutches," he says.

While most folks might consider his job dangerous, Kennemer views it as a competition between himself and the animals. "People ask me if I'm in rodeos, and I say, 'Well, I'm in one every day, but I don't have to pay to be in it,'" he says. "That animal is trying to kill you and you're trying to catch it, and I'm very competitive. I like the satisfaction of going out there and beating that animal."

By the time he takes care of the chores around his own ranch, including feeding cows, horses, and dogs, and training cattle dogs (his specialty), Kennemer often puts in 12-hour days. Still, he enjoys what he does, mostly because of the variety it offers. "I like being able to go to work at a different place every day," he says. "I don't have a boss and, if I don't like somebody, I don't have to go back, although that rarely happens."

Art Harris, one of his regular customers, says Kennemer does really good work. "He's dependable, fast, trustworthy, and efficient," says Harris, who owns more than 200 cows and also is CEO of a six-bank holding company headquartered in Elk City. "In this part of the country, it's pretty common to hire day workers, but they come and go, drifting from job to job. I feel like Kennemer is here to stay."

Indeed, Kennemer has a family to help support. Married to a school teacher and the father of two teenagers, Kennemer says they are fine with what he does for a living, although "my kids still haven't figured out what to put on the forms that ask for their dad's occupation."

The nature of the job is always changing. A couple of years ago, Kennemer added another cowboy service by building holding pens on his ranch to rest cattle on their way from Kentucky, Florida, and Tennessee to feed lots in the Texas Panhandle. They stay for five or six hours, getting food and water, before going on to be fattened up for the market. "I guess you could say I operate a bovine bed-and-breakfast," he says.

His father, grandfather, and great-grandfather farmed and ran cattle in Elk City before him, so Kennemer grew up around horses and cows. He earned a petroleum engineering degree from Oklahoma State University and worked for nine years for a well service company, first in Alaska and Louisiana, then throughout the mid-continent states from his home base of Elk City. He also taught high school in Elk City for four years before going full-time as a freelance cowboy in 1999. He says he prefers freelancing to owning cattle because he earns more money with less financial risk.

"I couldn't keep up with both jobs," Kennemer says of why he abandoned engineering and teaching. "Now I can't imagine making a living doing anything else."

—Elaine Hobson Miller

At the end of the day, success is about being honest and true to yourself and caring for your family.

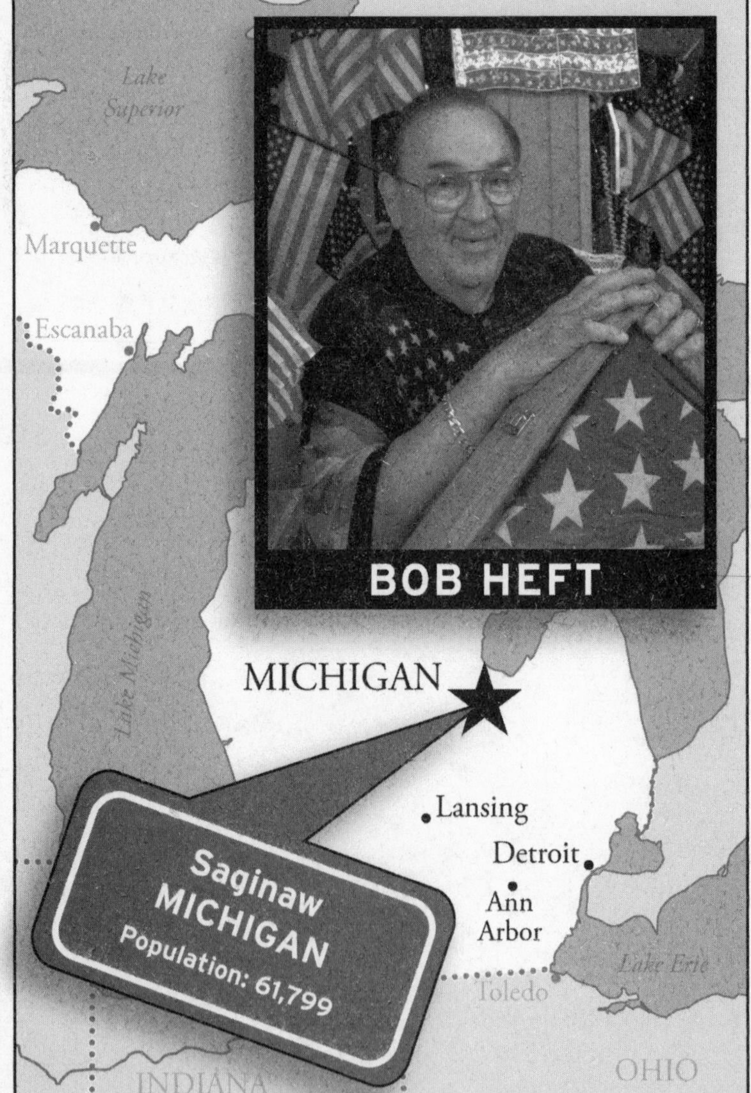

Lake Superior
Marquette
Escanaba
Lake Michigan
BOB HEFT
MICHIGAN
Lansing
Detroit
Ann Arbor
Lake Erie
Toledo
Saginaw
MICHIGAN
Population: 61,799
INDIANA
OHIO

New Stars for Old Glory

Bob Heft says a "B-minus" on his high school history project changed his life forever and ensured his place in history as the designer of America's 50-star flag.

It was 1958, and Heft was a 17-year-old student at Lancaster High School in Lancaster, Ohio, when teacher Stanley Pratt assigned a visual history project to his class. Heft, who had an interest in flags, was intrigued by the proposed addition of Alaska to the United States. He knew additional states would mean the nation must redesign its 48-star flag.

"I also knew that Alaska was a primarily Democratic state, so I figured that Congress would also want to add a Republican state before the 1960 [presidential] election," Heft says, referring to the addition of Hawaii. "So, I decided to make a model of a 50-star flag for my project."

Heft's grandmother, with whom he lived, was not pleased when her grandson began taking apart the family's American flag. Undeterred, he worked for more than 12 hours, painstakingly cutting out white stars and placing them onto a piece of blue broadcloth—50 stars on each side—then sewing the blue field back onto the red and white stripes. Because she thought he was mistreating the flag, she refused to help him; so Heft, who had never operated a sewing machine before, figured it out on his own.

"I'd never sewn before, and I've never sewn since," he chuckles.

Pleased with his efforts, he presented his flag project to the class. Mr. Pratt, however, was not as impressed. "It's got too many stars," he pointed out, giving the flag project a "B-minus." When Heft protested, the teacher challenged him: "If you don't like the grade, get this flag accepted in Washington, and I'll consider changing it."

Heft did just that. He took the flag to his congressman, U.S. Rep. Walter Moeller, and asked him, "If there's ever a contest for a new flag, would you submit this for me?"

Sure enough, Heft's political instincts proved true. Alaska was admitted as the nation's 49th state in 1959, and Hawaii as the 50th soon after. On July 4, 1960, Heft found himself in Washington, D.C., standing next to President Dwight Eisenhower, watching his 50-star flag raised for the first time over the U.S. Capitol building.

When he returned home with his flag, Heft sought out his former teacher, who gladly bumped up the grade to an "A." "If he hadn't given me that bad grade," Heft says, "I probably would have gone home and put the flag away. The lesson is, if you believe in what you're doing, don't let anyone dissuade you from your dreams."

Heft, 65, and his original 50-star flag have since traveled the world, sharing a message of patriotism. In fact, his original prototype has flown over all 50 state capitols, 131 American embassies, hundreds of historical sites, and the White House of every administration since Eisenhower. The flag is valued at more than $500,000.

Hoping to start college funds for his great-nephew and great-niece, Heft put the flag up for auction on eBay in 2005. While no one met his $250,000 reserve price, the auction listing received thousands of "hits" and generated much media attention. Several private collectors have expressed an interest in purchasing the flag, but Heft is adamant that his creation is properly displayed "where people can see it, and that it will be treated with respect."

For now, the flag stays with Heft and travels with him throughout the country. It rarely leaves its wood-and-glass case, but people can take a look at the blue field with the white stars that still bear the pencil marks where the young Heft sketched out his design.

Over the last 47 years, Heft estimates that he's made close to 9,000 appearances with his original 50-star flag, giving priority to scout groups, churches, military events, patriotic gatherings, fraternal organizations, and school assemblies and commencements.

"To the kids, he urged them to follow their dreams and never give up in what they believe in," said Larry Richardson, president of the Junior Achievement chapter in Lansing, Michigan. "Plus, he's sharing something unexpected. Most people never think about the fact that someone had to design the flag. People feel proud to be an American after they hear him."

During his career, Heft was a teacher for 23 years, including a stint at his high school alma mater, teaching a number of courses including history and government. He served as a seven-term mayor of Napoleon, Ohio, from 1976 to 1998. Now retired and living in Saginaw, Michigan, he makes approximately 250 appearances each year, often speaking for free and asking organizations to only cover his travel expenses. He estimates that he is on the road 150 days a year, sometimes speaking to four or five schools in a single day.

"I try to bring history to life and make it educational, entertaining, and inspirational," Heft says. "I especially try to spread my message to the younger generation, as I feel strongly that patriotism is needed in many of our schools. I also tell young people to believe in themselves."

—ELIZABETH JOHNSON

"If you believe in what you are doing, don't let anyone discourage you from your dreams."
—Bob Heft

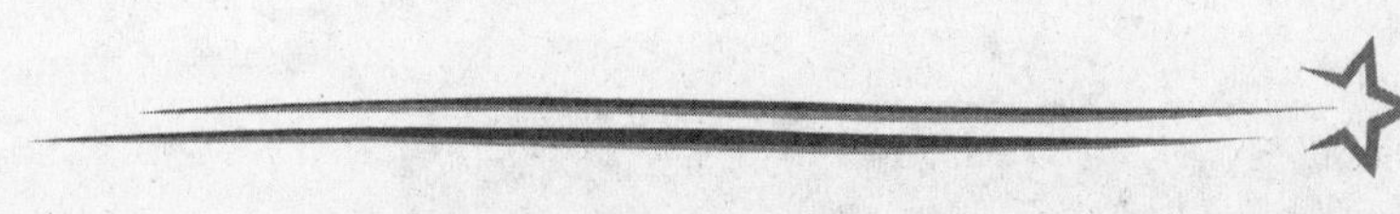

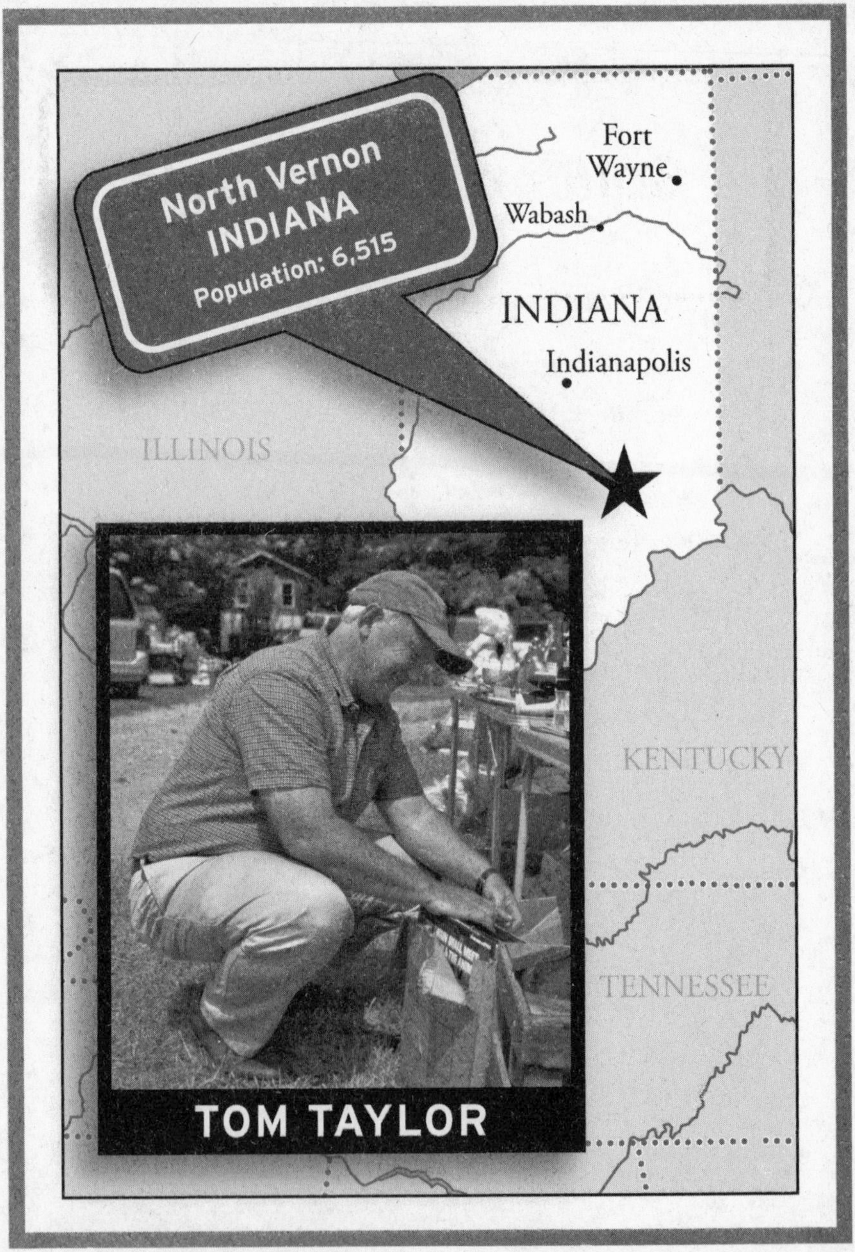

North Vernon
INDIANA
Population: 6,515

Fort Wayne
Wabash
INDIANA
Indianapolis
ILLINOIS
KENTUCKY
TENNESSEE

TOM TAYLOR

Sold on a Yard Sale

When Tom Taylor went yard sale shopping a few years ago around his home in North Vernon, Indiana, he bought an old DeSoto hubcap for $1. "I've never had a DeSoto and never will," the retired school administrator says. "It was just something I saw and wanted for the nostalgia."

Beyond the unlikely treasure, what Taylor remembers most from that yard sale experience was seeing all the happy people selling things they no longer wanted—and the equally happy people who were buying them. That was his goal when he dreamed up the Great U.S. 50 Yard Sale in 1999.

"My idea was that for one special weekend every year, people can hop in their cars, drive to Highway 50, turn right or left, and go yard sale hunting," says Taylor, 59. "That is the fun."

From his Indiana home, Taylor volunteers his time promoting U.S. 50 as the mecca for yard sale enthusiasts each weekend before Memorial Day.

The first sale was held in 2000, and the momentum has built every year since. "One guy stopped me on the street not long ago and thanked me," Taylor says. "He said that he had made $1,100 selling things he no longer needed. That made me happy."

As national coordinator of the coast-to-coast event, Taylor envisioned a gigantic yard sale stretching from sea to shining sea along U.S. Highway 50, which courses 3,200 miles through a dozen states, four state capitals, and the nation's capital en route from Ocean City, Maryland, to Sacramento, California.

Taylor's idea was launched following a meeting with Susan Walters, Jennings County tourism director, and Barbara King, publisher of the *North Vernon Plain Dealer*. The group was searching for ways to promote tourism and help bring money to local communities in southeastern Indiana and rural residents feeling the crunch of a tight economy. What he didn't want, Taylor says, was something that relied on government aid, grant writing, committees, and a zillion meetings. Throw in the idea of recycling reusable items, and the great yard sale was a natural solution.

To expand the idea beyond his neck of the woods, Taylor traveled Highway 50 via the World Wide Web and tracked down communities and their leaders. "It's just a matter of finding phone numbers and making calls," he says. "Usually I would start with the tourism office. If they didn't have one of those, I would go for the chamber of commerce. If they didn't have that, I would go to the local newspaper. I just kept going until I found somebody."

Once he connected with local officials, Taylor was surprised at how easy it all became. "You just tell people when and where the yard sales are going to be and they take it from there," Taylor says. "Sometimes people don't decide until the last minute that they are going to do it. Maybe it rains and they decide they won't. Or maybe the sun is shining and they decide they will. You never know until it happens. But there are always enough yard sales to make it all worthwhile."

Taylor fell in love with the historic U.S. 50 while growing up in North Vernon, a few blocks from the old two-lane highway that spans America. "It crosses mountains and deserts, as well as farmland," he says, unfolding a U.S. 50 brochure from the 1950s. "I wanted people to get off the big interstates and see the 'real' America."

Within just a few short years, that is exactly what was happening on a recent weekend sale. "It's been a steady stream here ever since we opened this morning," Bernadine Hunter said as shoppers browsed through odds and ends at her home along U.S. 50 near Bedford, Indiana.

Up the road in Brownstown, Indiana, Todd Darlage and his group of six families had sold about $1,200 worth of merchandise by 2 P.M. Darlage busily unloaded boxes and arranged items on makeshift tables, clotheslines, and tarps spread on the ground. Shoppers eagerly followed after him, picking up bargains before they were even displayed.

Across the nation, some local governments have pitched in by waiving yard sale fees, providing police assistance and clean-up crews, donating fairgrounds and public sites for the sale, and giving free publicity for the annual event. "I do like the spirit of our country when it comes to people coming together to do things," Taylor says.

In Las Animas, Colorado, the city and county organized a yard sale at the Bent County Fairgrounds, right off U.S. 50. It was a "grassroots" project with no money charged for setting up and no red tape to wade through, says Kathryn Finau, executive director of the Bent County Development Foundation. County commissioners allowed the fairgrounds to be used free of charge, the sheriff's department sent out a county jail work crew to set up, and the *Bent County Democrat* publicized the event.

"Route 50 goes right through the middle of town and we had people coming from all over the valley," Finau says. "All the neighboring counties came to see what was going on. It was fantastic. I'm so glad Tom Taylor started it."

In Nevada, U.S. 50 is known as "the loneliest road in America," says Larry Osborne of the Carson City Chamber of Commerce. But the yard sale still attracts many sellers and buyers. "Highway 50 runs right through Carson City, but when you can drive 100 miles between communities on a highway, that makes it a little more difficult."

But it also makes it part of the fun. "The coast-to-coast concept is really symbolic," Taylor says. "Obviously, there are mountains and deserts where the event will not be table to table. But I have this vision of some yard sale out in Utah that has a sign in the yard 'Last Yard Sale for 83 Miles.' I think that would be great."

—Jackie Sheckler Finch

When we identify our collective strengths and join together, we can turn a lonely highway into a treasured slice of Americana.

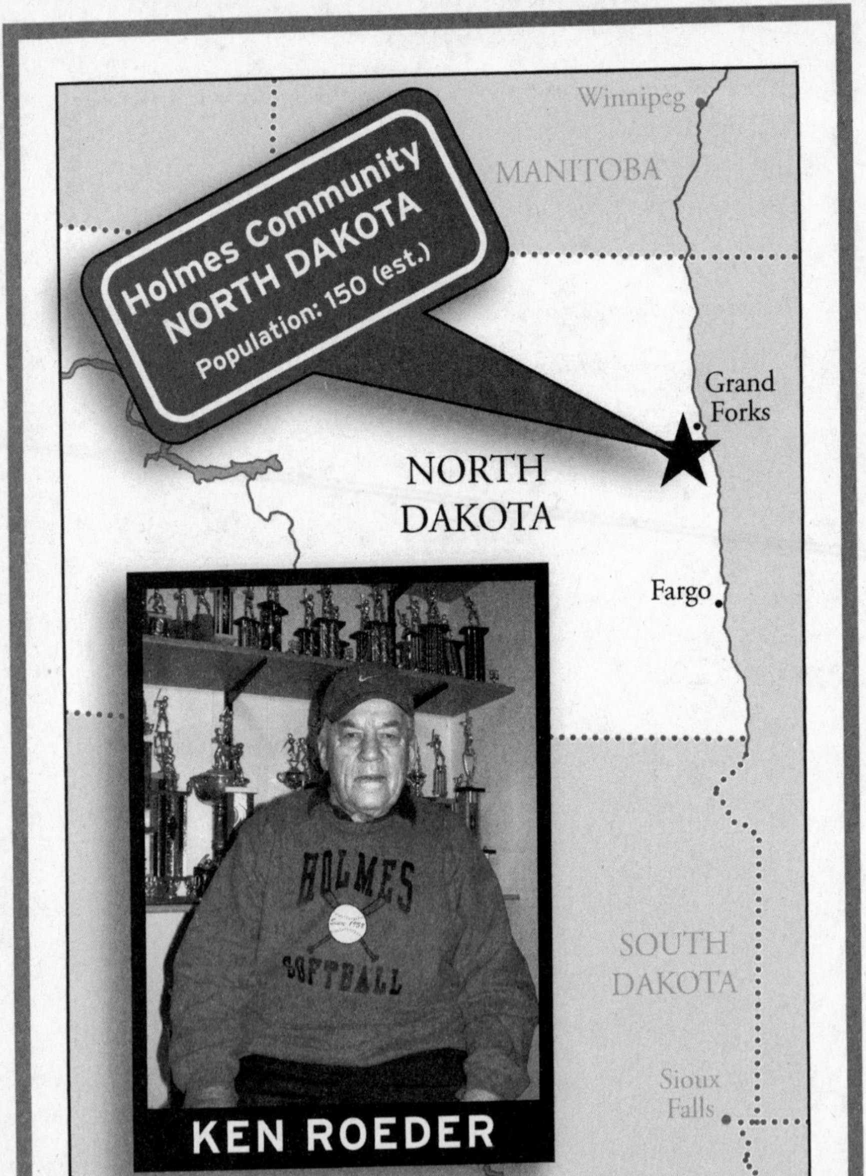

Holmes Community
NORTH DAKOTA
Population: 150 (est.)

Winnipeg

MANITOBA

Grand Forks

NORTH DAKOTA

Fargo

SOUTH DAKOTA

Sioux Falls

HOLMES SOFTBALL

KEN ROEDER

Field of Dreams

Just off the gravel road where the town's general store once stood, a narrow dirt trail is marked by a solitary street sign: Ken Roeder Drive. On summer evenings, dust rises as cars follow the tree-framed trail to a grassy clearing dominated by a manicured ball diamond surrounded by fields of soybeans.

Ken Roeder, 81, is always there. Roeder is the general manager and driving force that has kept softball alive for more than half a century in Holmes, a farming community 20 miles southwest of Grand Forks, North Dakota.

Until 1992, Roeder was still playing. Knee problems prevent him from running bases anymore—he finally had knee replacement surgery in 2006—but that hasn't stopped him from showing up at every game and continuing his roles as honorary coach and jack-of-all-trades.

Fans fill the bleachers, and children play on the swings Roeder helped build. The smell of hot dogs wafts from the concession stand he manages.

Without Roeder, softball would have died in Holmes years ago.

"Kenny is the reason there's a ball diamond here and the reason we're still playing," says the Rev. Mark Ellingson, a member of the Holmes team and pastor of the Holmes United Methodist Church, where Roeder has been a member most of his life.

A retired dairy farmer, Roeder began playing on a makeshift ball field near Holmes when he was 5 years old. "We only lived a couple miles from here," recalls Roeder, who typically played pitcher or catcher. "I liked the game right away. But after a while, I got tired of playing in a cow pasture, and I thought we had enough interest to have a real ballpark."

In the early 1950s, Roeder approached Ralph Schroeder and asked the landowner to donate the pasture for a real ball diamond. When Schroeder agreed, Roeder rallied other players to volunteer time and equipment to build a diamond.

Over the years, he raised money to buy lights for the field, mowed the grass, dragged the diamond, got Coca-Cola to donate a scoreboard, enlisted help to build modern restrooms to replace the outhouse, and coached many of the teams.

"If you're going to find something going on around here, it's always been the diamond or the church," says Bud Fitchner, a former player and longtime friend of Roeder's. "That very first year when we put in the diamond, concession stand, and bleachers, the people started coming. That never changed. Now, concessions and our annual social are the ways we make money to pay for things we need."

Most folks at Holmes United Methodist Church are also players and fans for the Holmes softball team. The country church is a quarter of a mile from the ball field and the closest church to town, so it's a natural gathering spot to display the team's 90 or so trophies and hold the group's annual softball dinner and fund-raiser.

"I've gotten to know a lot of the young guys in church and they come to play ball with us," says Roeder. "When you have things in common like that, you don't really notice the difference in age, and these young people can talk to me about things. It's kind of nice."

As the town's population has waned, the number of teams has decreased to seven—organized informally by groups of area residents who love to play ball. Still, the Holmes team maintains its reputation for good ballplayers and frequently competes in state tournaments.

"A lot of the guys play because they want to play for Kenny," Ellingson says. "Ken keeps this community close-knit, not just with his love of the game, but with his love of people and the way he reaches out to everyone around here. He's a walking welcome wagon. He is the one person who keeps this diamond going."

Player Brian Schneider and his family were newcomers still unpacking their belongings when Roeder showed up at their door. "Kenny pitched in and helped us. Then he invited us to play ball," says Schneider, whose 18-year-old son, Wade, also plays. "This is where Kenny's heart is. It's a real ministry for him."

Roeder, uncomfortable with praise and a man of few words, says it's probably time to quit. Then he adds, "Of course, we have a good T-ball team coming up, and I'm hoping we'll get a girls' team going again. We kind of ran out of girls."

In 1998, Roeder was inducted into the North Dakota Softball Hall of Fame after being nominated by people in the Holmes area. While induction ceremonies are traditionally held during state softball tournaments, tradition was abandoned as hundreds gathered at the Holmes ballpark for Roeder's induction ceremony.

"If you build it, they will come," proclaimed the baseball movie *Field of Dreams*. Ken Roeder is proof of that.

—Candi Helseth

The camaraderie forged on a dusty ball field cuts through all barriers.

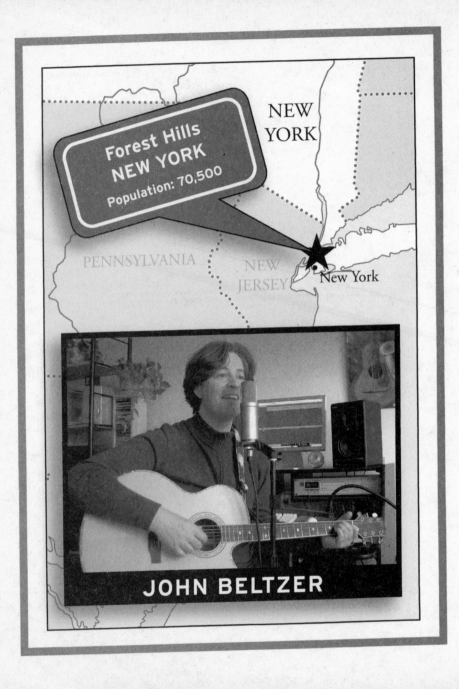

Forest Hills
NEW YORK
Population: 70,500
NEW YORK
PENNSYLVANIA
NEW JERSEY
New York
JOHN BELTZER

Songs of Love

Singer and songwriter John Beltzer was at a professional crossroads in 1996 when he came up with an idea that's helped thousands of chronically and terminally ill children.

"I had just lost a record deal and was pretty devastated," explains Beltzer, 47, of Forest Hills, New York. "I was walking down the street in my neighborhood and had an epiphany to use my talents for a higher purpose."

After years of attempting to write jazzy and alternative pop songs that he hoped would be adored by millions, Beltzer saw far greater potential in writing for significantly smaller audiences—one child at a time. "The concept just popped into my head to write personalized songs for seriously ill children," he says. "It was such a simple yet powerful idea, but something told me nobody had done it before."

Beltzer contacted St. Jude Children's Hospital in Memphis, Tennessee, and over a four-day period wrote and recorded six personalized songs for six kids based on biographical information provided by hospital staff. "I just knew it was going to work," he says.

Two weeks later, he got a call from the mother of Brittany Smith, one of the first children to receive a personalized song. "She put Brittany on the phone who, with the cutest little voice, said, 'Thank you for my song.' I hung up and cried for half an hour.

"I knew that call was all the Grammy award I was ever going to need."

More than a decade later, the Songs of Love Foundation has enlisted more than 500 professional songwriters to write and record customized songs for more than 10,000 seriously ill children across the nation. Beltzer has written about 1,000 songs himself. Celebrities, including Michael Bolton, Billy Joel, Ronnie Spector, David Lee Roth, Nancy Sinatra, and the Broadway cast of *Titanic* also have volunteered their talents. Currently producing about 220 songs a month, the organization has a full-time staff of four, plus three part-time employees based in Forest Hills.

The process starts when a family member or caregiver fills out and submits a Songs of Love profile form, downloaded from the foundation's Web site at *www.songsoflove.org* or provided by the hospital. The child's name, interests, and hobbies, as well as names of friends, pets, and family members, are then integrated into a song written just for him or her, professionally recorded and delivered on cassette or CD to the child's bedside. Turnaround for a customized song is typically four to eight weeks, but can be as little as 24 to 48 hours in dire circumstances. Costs and overhead average about $250 per song, but there's no charge to families; expenses are underwritten by private and corporate donations. Requests grew by 21 percent last year, however, and funding continues to be a challenge.

Nancy Harrison of Oklahoma City, Oklahoma, requested a song in 2005 for her 5-year-old grandson Mikey, who's battling lymphoma. "He had just started a really tough treatment," Harrison says. "School was starting and he didn't want to go because he didn't have any hair. We surprised him with the song and he lit up like a candle. We were all crying. It really gave him some kind of power."

Six-year-old Betsi Kennedy of Madison, Wisconsin, received her Song of Love while undergoing chemotherapy for a brain tumor in 2005. "We can't get it out of her CD player," says Betsi's mom, Debi Kennedy. A year later, Betsi still listens to it, and the song remains a source of strength. "Receiving this song," Kennedy says, "has been like a ray of sunshine at just the right time."

—Chuck Aly

When disappointment comes, be open-minded to new directions and possibilities. "Failure" may lead to a greater purpose and ultimate success.

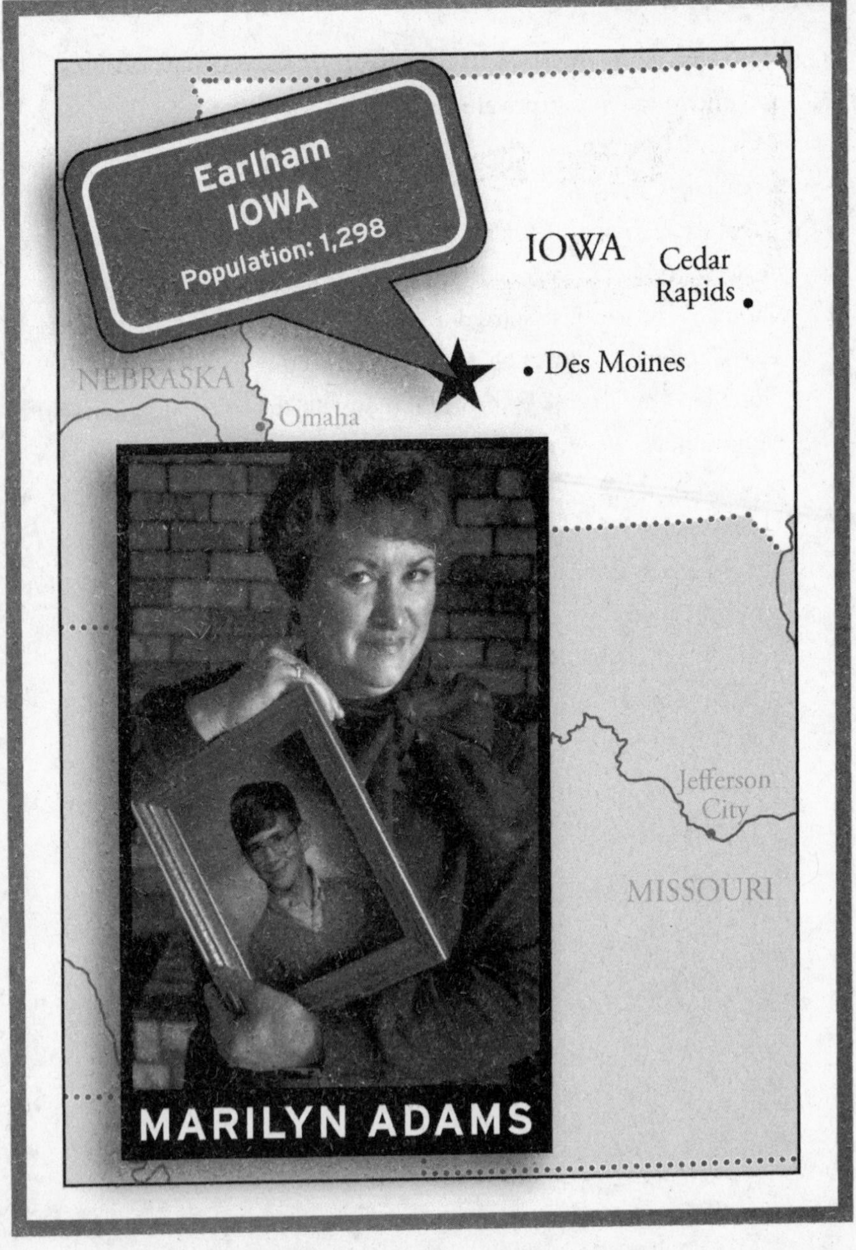

Earlham
IOWA
Population: 1,298

IOWA
Cedar Rapids
Des Moines
NEBRASKA
Omaha
Jefferson City
MISSOURI

MARILYN ADAMS

One Son's Legacy

Marilyn Adams of Earlham, Iowa, was in shock for months after losing her 11-year-old son, Keith Algreen, in a farming accident in 1986. As Adams rebuilt her shattered life, she and her daughter, Kelly, began a local campaign to safeguard other children from farm-related accidents.

Within a year of her son's death, Adams founded a national organization aimed at promoting farm safety and preventing future tragedies. In 2007, Farm Safety 4 Just Kids (FS4JK) celebrates its 20th anniversary of teaching about the risks children face when playing on or operating farm machinery.

Adams learned that painful lesson when her son stayed home from school on October 15, 1986, to help with the harvest. Keith's dad, Darrell, was running a combine in the field, while Keith's job was to run the auger that moved corn into a storage bin from a side door in the wagon that his dad filled.

"For some reason Keith got up in the wagon while it was unloading," Adams says. "The gravity-flow wagon worked like quicksand, pulling him to the bottom. When Darrell got back, he saw that Keith was missing and the wagon was mostly full. He ended up pulling Keith out from underneath 2 tons of corn and driving him to the local clinic. Keith was soon Life-Flighted to the nearest hospital. Twenty-four hours later, they took Keith off life support."

Healing came in the form of a project for FFA (formerly Future Farmers of America) pursued by Kelly, then a senior at Earlham Community School. Kelly wanted to do a speech about her little brother's accident and needed a demonstration model. Her dad made a working model of the wagon using unpopped popcorn kernels and a toy person to demonstrate the danger. Her mom helped with the research.

"It gave me something positive to focus on," Adams says.

Soon after, Adams decided to design a warning decal for gravity-flow wagons. Media attention and funding from the University of Iowa allowed her to establish the nonprofit FS4JK in October 1987, approximately one year after her son's death.

The wagon model spawned the organization's safety resource catalog, which features puppet shows, skits, videos, puzzles, posters, and safety educational packets. Today, FS4JK has 131 chapters in 36 states and four Canadian provinces. Additional volunteers belong to a network of partnerships including the Farm Service

Agency and agricultural corporations. The organization also has paid part-time outreach coordinators in five states with plans to expand that network.

Volunteers do everything from lobbying for safety shields on machinery to conducting hazard hunts and farm safety day camps for kids. In 2005, the chapter network reached more than 1 million children, youth, and farm families through more than 870 activities with 6,530 volunteers donating 63,000 hours of their time.

"I take great pride in the fact that we are working as the voice for rural children," Adams says.

Adams believes the program is saving lives. From 1982 to 1989—the period when Keith died—an average of 181 youths under age 20 were killed annually on farms, compared with 103 deaths annually between 1990 and 1996, according to a report for the National Institute for Occupational Safety and Health. The report, which offers the most recent data available, shows a 43 percent drop in annual farm-related deaths of children and youth during those time periods.

Most accidents are attributed to unsupervised children, children tackling tasks inappropriate for their age or ability, and parents unaware that some traditional farming practices are highly dangerous—the same dangers FS4JK continues to warn about through education.

"Education and awareness are all the tools we need to work with," says Adams. "We would like parents to utilize guidelines and make lists to put on their refrigerators with their rules and then enforce these rules on their farm."

This organization has helped many families who have lost children on the farm, including Cindy and Jeff Gerard of Pittsfield, Illinois. They had warned 6-year-old Colin to stay away from a tractor being used to grind hog feed. But in 1995, in the few minutes that Jeff left to answer the phone, Colin became entangled in the machinery and died. The Gerards joined FS4JK several months later. Cindy has been president of the western Illinois chapter since 1996, and the couple has created four more Illinois chapters.

"This helped us channel our pain in a positive manner," says Cindy.

In 1997, she gave birth to another son, Austin, now 8. "He can, of course, never take the place of Colin, but he gives us a reason to smile again," says Cindy. "Austin has been going to the farm safety day camps since he was a baby, and I am always surprised by what he picks up. One time he saw a bunch of high school kids riding in the back of a pickup and he said to me, 'They shouldn't be doing that, should they, Mom?'"

Adams is grateful for—and empathizes with—parents such as the Gerards and is hopeful that together they can make farms safer for children, including her 3-year-old grandson by daughter Kelly, now 38 and a full-time mom.

"At some point in the healing process I realized I couldn't bring Keith back," Adams says. "So the second best thing I can do is use our family as an example to help prevent other children from losing their lives."

—Karen Karvonen

Turning the tragic loss of human life into triumphs that safeguard and improve the lives of others can be our greatest testament to the power of love.

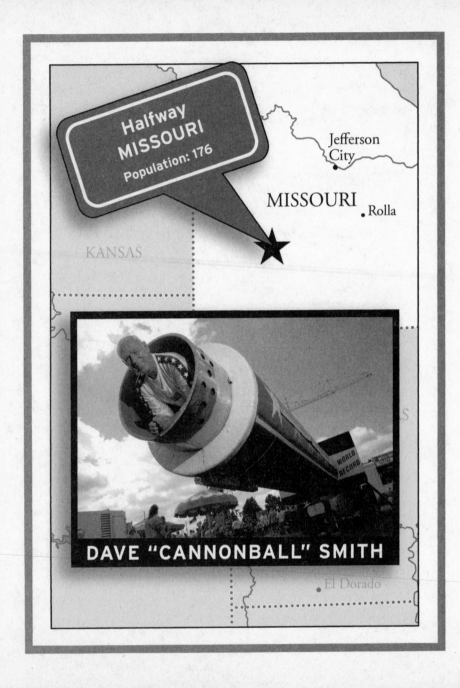

Halfway
MISSOURI
Population: 176

Jefferson City

MISSOURI

Rolla

KANSAS

DAVE "CANNONBALL" SMITH

El Dorado

Having a Blast

Dave "Cannonball" Smith, 64, kneels at the opening of his 33-foot-long, star-spangled cannon. As the barrel elevates, he waves to the crowd at the Steele County Free Fair in Owatonna, Minnesota, and slips into the steel cocoon that's aimed toward a net 145 feet away. But first he must soar 60 feet into the air and pass over two Ferris wheels.

The crowd counts down: "five, four, three, two, one!" With a loud boom and a cloud of smoke, Smith hurtles out of the cannon. The force of 9 Gs blurs his vision and distorts his body until he eventually tucks his head and flips onto his back to prepare for landing. As he hits the net, he quickly grabs hold to keep from ricocheting off. Fortunately, Smith's nearly 4-second flight ends safely with thunderous applause.

"I was dazed and amazed," says Joe Slezinger, a Chicago resident who witnessed Smith's aerial performance last year. "It's scary enough just sitting on a Ferris wheel, protected by a bar from falling out. It boggles the mind that he flew over the top of the Ferris wheel with no protection from being killed if he misses the net."

For the 30-year cannonball veteran, it's all in a day's work. "I've learned to live with the fears and emotions," says Smith, who gives two dozen performances each summer, spending the remainder of the year at his 50-acre farm near Halfway, Missouri.

"It's a very rewarding profession," he says. "I have little kids wrap their arms around me and say, 'I love you.' They want to touch and talk to me. I enjoy making people happy."

Smith's high-flying career launched in 1970 when he joined a traveling circus as a catcher in a trapeze act. Ambitious to star as a solo act, he designed and perfected a human-launching cannon in his spare time.

In 1975, he took to the air, performing his first show in Saginaw, Michigan. Since then he's meticulously recorded the angles, humidity, distance, and temperature of thousands of his shots. "The gun is very accurate," he says. "Given certain conditions, I can go right where I want." Of course, that doesn't mean it's not dangerous. "I have just the length of the barrel to accelerate enough to go the distance I want. There's enough power to turn me into peanut butter if anything went wrong."

Smith's daughter, Jennifer Schneider, of Boliver, Missouri, grew up watching her father perform as the human cannonball at corporate conventions, fairs, and amusement parks. "It was just what my dad was," she says. "I didn't think it was strange until I was older. Then I did it, too."

Schneider, who goes by the nickname "Cannon Lady," is among

three of Smith's 10 children who are professional cannonballs, using cannons built by Smith.

The family performs together for special events such as appearances on the *Today Show* and *The Tonight Show with Jay Leno.* Otherwise, their separate careers take them around the world. Jennifer works at motocross events in the United States; Stephanie stars in Australia as "Lady Cannon"; and Dave Smith Jr., known as "The Bullet," has blasted across the Grand Canyon and often performs in the Middle East.

In 1998, both father and son broke the 1940 record for the longest human cannonball flight, launching simultaneously in Pennsylvania's Kennywood Park. Dave Jr. landed first at just over 181 feet, besting the 1940 record by 7 inches. A split second later, Dave Sr. outdistanced his son with a 185-foot, 10-inch flight, which stands as the world record.

"I live for those kinds of moments," the elder Smith says.

When he's not performing, Smith usually can be found at his Missouri farm, where his barn holds farming equipment, as well as a trampoline, trapeze, and a gym for off-season training.

"I'm doing something I like," he says. "A lot of people can't do that. I won't stop until I keel over."

—Vicki Cox

Find a job that you love, and do it with precision and joy, and the rest will come.

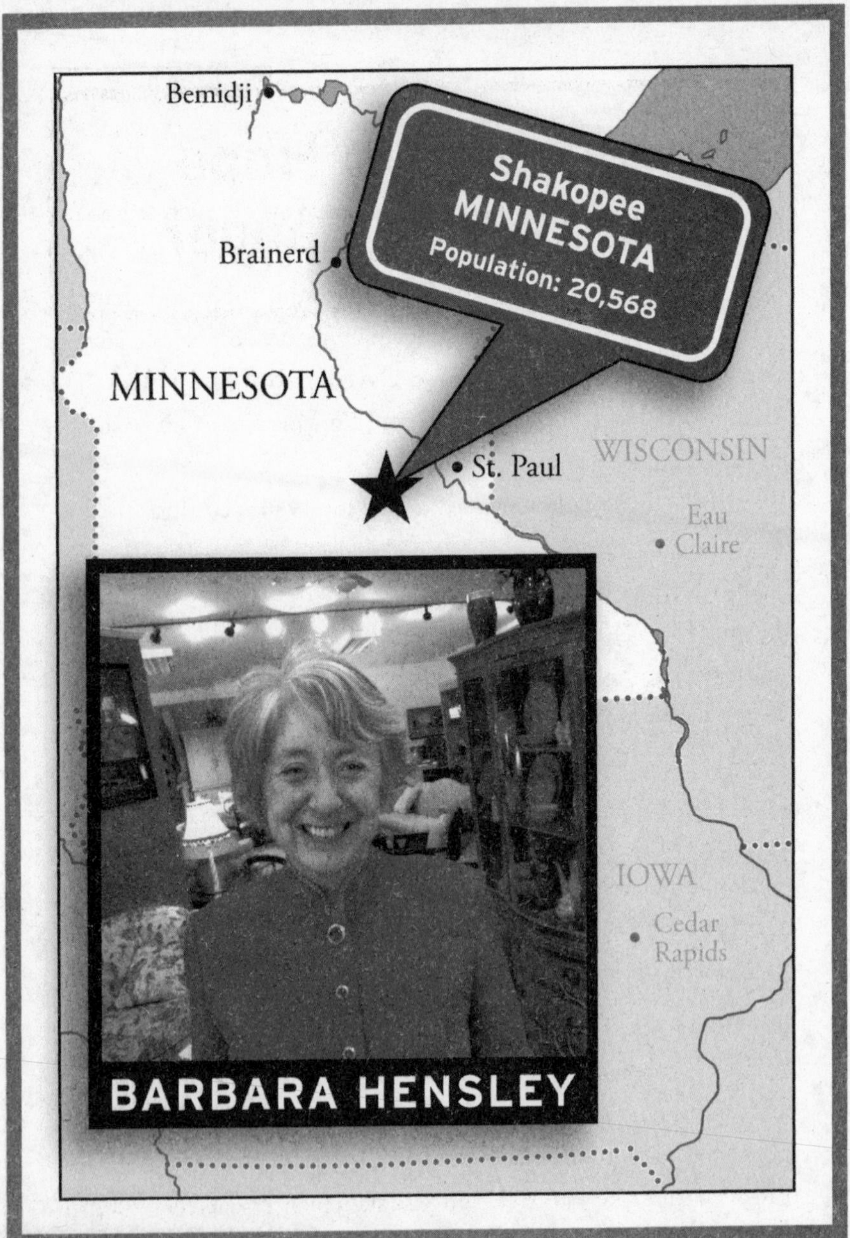

Shakopee
MINNESOTA
Population: 20,568

Bemidji
Brainerd
MINNESOTA
St. Paul
WISCONSIN
Eau Claire
IOWA
Cedar Rapids

BARBARA HENSLEY

Generating Hope for Breast Cancer

When Barbara Hensley decided to leave her corporate job in 2001, retirement was the furthest thing from her mind. Hensley, of Shakopee, Minnesota, had lost two sisters to breast cancer and her plan was to help others with the disease.

Using marketing experience she'd gained while working as an executive throughout the years, Hensley decided to help raise money for breast cancer programs while enabling other women to become what she calls "social entrepreneurs."

"I carefully researched other foundations and decided the best way to raise money was to open stores where women could be successful entrepreneurs and at the same time they would be able to give back to their community," says Hensley, 59.

So she asked companies and individuals to donate overstocked and used items to sell in an upscale store. The result was a nonprofit foundation named Hope Chest for Breast Cancer and a for-profit retail store called Hope Chest, which opened in 2002 in

Orono, Minnesota, and has contributed more than $200,000 to breast cancer causes.

What sets the 6,000-square-foot Hope Chest store apart from other stores is that each day customers can find something different among the merchandise, from a sterling silver tea set and ornate wooden frames, to an 1890s oak table and high-end clothing.

Julie Riff, one of 200 Hope Chest volunteers, says Hensley is an inspiration. "Barbara is incredibly dedicated to the Hope Chest mission," Riff says. "She's always positive and sincere and has created a great place to work. I think her work ethic and unflagging enthusiasm and graciousness have inspired me the most."

Kari Berscheit, a breast cancer survivor, also volunteers at the Hope Chest store. "I always enjoy working there and I can't believe all these items are donated," Berscheit says. "I just love Barbara."

While many cancer charities raise money for one specific purpose, Hope Chest donates money to four different areas—research, hospice care, financial support to those with breast cancer, and programs for early detection.

Hensley believes that helping people with breast cancer meet financial burdens, such as paying medical bills and living expenses, is crucial. "When both my sisters were going through treatment, I got to meet women who sometimes had to put off taking chemotherapy because they had inadequate or no insurance," she says.

Financial aid given by Hope Chest often means a breast cancer patient can buy food or even pay rent. One example is a donation to the Western Communities Action Network, a social service center that aids low-income families in Mound, Minnesota.

"We had one client who was a single mom and taking chemotherapy," says Jessie Billiet, a family advocate with the network. "She needed some help paying her mortgage, so we contacted Barbara and she sent a donation which allowed the client to stay in her home."

Ultimately, Hensley hopes to expand the Hope Chest concept by establishing stores in all 50 states, which combined would raise an estimated $10 million annually. In 2006, she opened the second Hope Chest store in St. Paul, Minnesota, and became licensed to offer franchise opportunities in all 50 states.

"Doing what I am is important to me because I lost the dearest women in my life," says Hensley, whose sisters Kathy and Patsy died in 1994 and 1996, respectively. "One day I'd love to be sitting on my front porch surrounded by my great-grandchildren. They'll ask me what I did with my life, and I'll say I had the opportunity to work with wonderful people to help fight breast cancer. And they'll look up at me and ask, 'What's breast cancer?'"

—Susan Palmquist

One way to defeat personal tragedy is to relentlessly pursue hope for others.

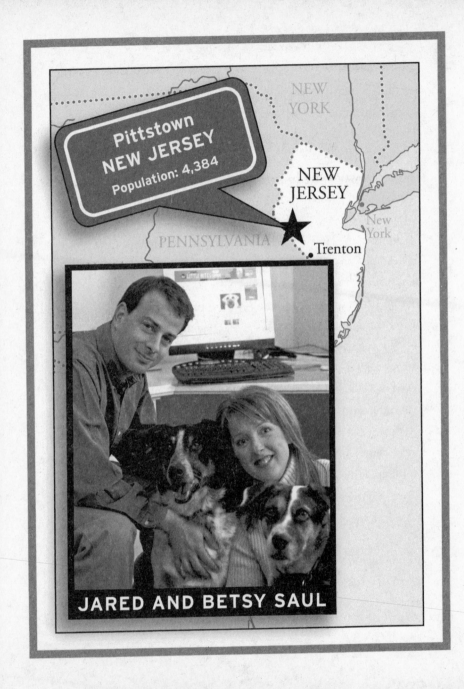

Pittstown
NEW JERSEY
Population: 4,384

NEW YORK

NEW JERSEY

PENNSYLVANIA

New York

Trenton

JARED AND BETSY SAUL

Petfinders Extraordinaire

Maisey's green eyes beckon in the photo of her online profile. She likes quiet conversation, has a charming personality, and enjoys cuddling. She's even housebroken.

The gray tabby cat is among 230,000 homeless pets seeking human companions at Petfinder.com, a searchable database of cats, dogs, chickens, rabbits, horses, hamsters, pigs, iguanas, llamas, and more at 10,000 animal shelters nationwide.

Thanks to Jared and Betsy Saul of Pittstown, New Jersey, founders of Petfinder.com, these animals have a face and a voice. The matchmakers have been responsible for more than 10 million pet adoptions in the past decade.

"They're pioneers and innovators," says Rich Avanzino, an animal-welfare advocate in Alameda, California. "The beauty of Petfinder is that it levels the playing field for grassroots shelters in small towns with the big metropolitan shelters."

This means that Clinker, a congenial bluetick coonhound in off-the-beaten-path Mountainburg, Arkansas, gets the same exposure and chance of finding a home as a big-city hound when more than 6 million people visit Petfinder.com each month.

The Sauls started Petfinder.com in December 1995 as a New Year's resolution to help homeless animals. They were driving to dinner and discussing ways to use the Internet. "I said, 'You know this could be huge for animal shelters,'" says Betsy, 39, who always has had a tender heart for animals. At age 12, she spent her weekends volunteering with an animal-rescue group where she grew up in Joplin, Missouri.

The Sauls envisioned a free online database where people could find and adopt pets from shelters and animal rescue groups. Jared, a radiologist at Hunterdon Medical Center in Flemington, New Jersey, was in medical school at the time. He had been teaching himself computer languages since age 13 and was up to speed on the technology.

Betsy had goose bumps when they vowed to create their matchmaking Web site, imagining how many people could find loving companions. That weekend, Jared wrote a computer program for the service and Betsy started contacting shelters in New Jersey. They didn't have a fax machine, but a neighbor lent his so that 13 shelters in the state could provide information on animals available for adoption. Betsy typed in the information and scanned photos to post on the Web site.

"We began receiving testimonials from the shelters and adopters right away," says Jared, 37. By the end of the year, a thousand people were visiting the site daily and shelters reported that adoptions were skyrocketing because of the site. More and more shelters were becoming members.

In 1998, the Sauls decided to expand the service to animal shelters nationwide. Betsy gave up her job as an urban forester to run Petfinder.com full time. The couple set a lofty goal: to arrange 5 million animal adoptions within five years.

People can search for a pet by kind, breed, size, age, or location. Each animal has a snapshot and background story, if known, with a personality description. Some animals end up in shelters as a result of the owner's lifestyle change, such as a divorce, relocation, or move to a nursing home. Others have been abused or abandoned.

Adoption fees vary with each shelter and may cover medical treatment and other expenses. Petfinder.com doesn't charge adopters or shelters, but is supported by advertisers including Purina and PETCO.

"For the service to be free, it's just fabulous," says Bambi Haywood, president of the King George Animal Rescue League in King George, Virginia. "We could not exist without Petfinder." Volunteer rescuers in the village of 450 organized in 1998 and foster animals in their homes until they are adopted. "We get a lot of puppies and we post them online, and we get calls from as far south as Florida and as far north as Vermont," Haywood says.

Natasha Kemp of Cookeville, Tennessee, planned to spend several hundred dollars for a pricey purebred pup until she heard about Petfinder.com. "I hadn't even thought about a shelter dog," Kemp says. Then she clicked and stared into the eyes of a fluffy white dog at the Humane Association of Wilson County in Lebanon, Tennessee. "I found myself going back to his picture over and over again," says Kemp. "Here was this little dog who just wanted one person to want him."

Two hours before the shelter closed, she drove an hour to see him. "He's absolutely adorable," Kemp says about Charley, the wheaten-terrier mix she adopted for $75. "He loves swimming in the lake and walking in the park. Life without Charley is unthinkable."

The number of miles between the adopter and the adored pet usually isn't a problem. Sharon Shadduck of Vestal, New York, and her daughter, Olivia, searched for a dog after their Labrador retriever, Jake, died of cancer. They set their hearts on finding a Great Pyrenees and even settled on his name, Luca.

A few months into their search, Shadduck opened an e-mail from Petfinder.com and couldn't believe her eyes. "There he was—a 5-month-old pure Pyrenees already named Luca," Shadduck says. The puppy was 850 miles away at Jennifer's Rescues in Chattanooga, Tennessee, but Shadduck made the 15-hour drive to pick up the family's new pet.

"I knew the minute I saw him that he was the one," she says.

The Sauls are heartened that so many homeless animals are getting the attention and affection they deserve. "All these animals are waiting to enrich our lives," Jared says. "They're good companions. Kids who have a hard time bonding get help with a pet. People heal faster with pets."

Like millions of other pet lovers, the Sauls have opened their own hearts and home to animals whose profiles were posted on Petfinder.com. The couple's 65-acre farm is home to a menagerie, including four elderly horses, Dot, Harper, Mort, and Tina; a blind pony, Pony Baloney; two goats, Biscuit and Macy; a sheep, Angus; and two dogs, Kobie and Sophie.

Caring for the pets is a welcome break for Betsy after directing 25 employees across the United States from her home-based office. Petfinder.com, which has grown into a multimillion-dollar business through the sale of online advertising and merchandising, now employs computer programmers and Web designers, help-desk people, and staff members who work with animal shelters, corporate sponsors, and the media.

After a long day at the computer, Betsy leads her 37-year-old crippled horse, Dot, from the barn to a spacious pasture. "Look how straight this girl is walking," she brags.

When Betsy finishes feeding the animals, she plops on the floor to rest, and Kobie scrambles onto her lap where he gets smothered with kisses. The dog gazes at Betsy with adoring eyes.

It's another perfect match, courtesy of Petfinder.com.

—Marti Attoun

When we merge brilliant ideas with the soft spots in our hearts, it can make a difference for others—sometimes even for millions of people and their loving companions.

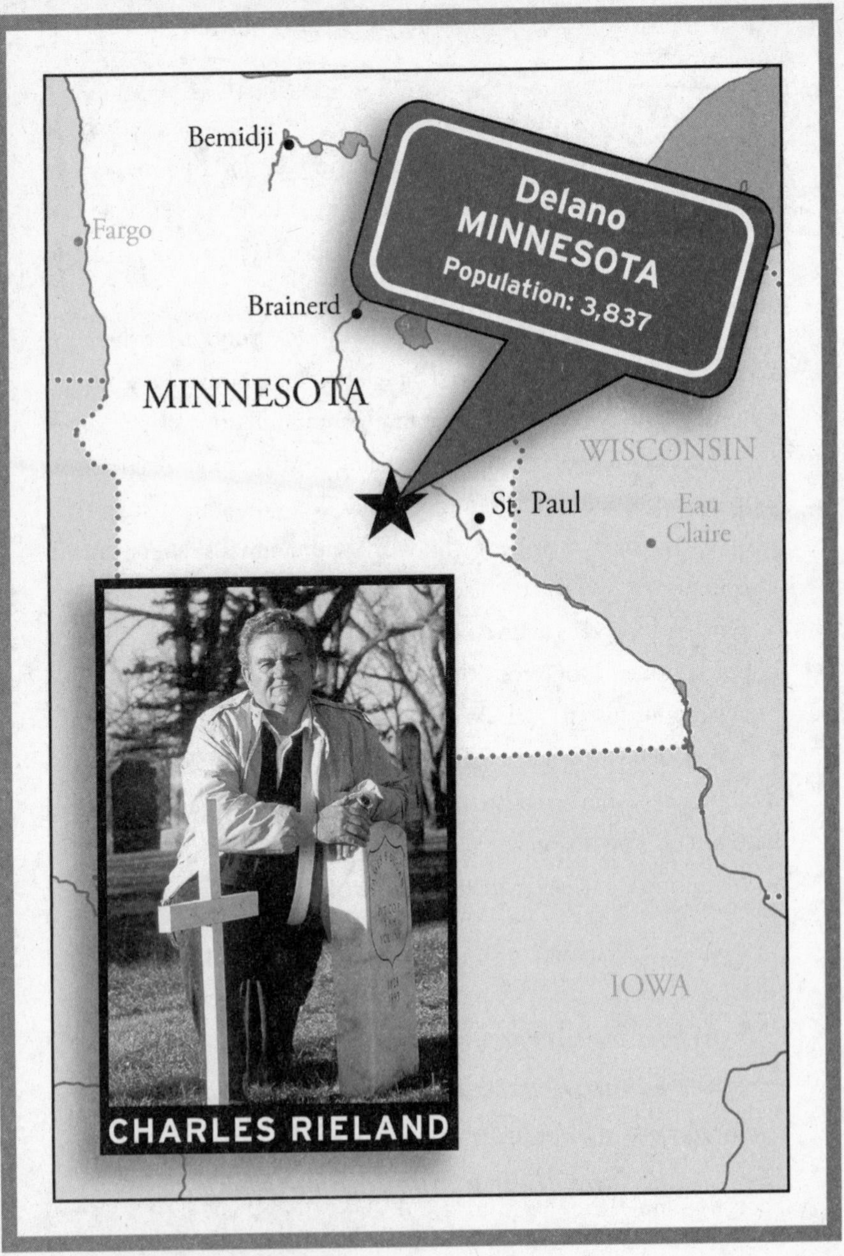

Bemidji
Fargo
Brainerd
MINNESOTA
Delano
MINNESOTA
Population: 3,837
WISCONSIN
St. Paul
Eau Claire
IOWA

CHARLES RIELAND

Cemetery Sleuth with a Cause

Driven by a deep respect for human life, Charles Rieland has made it his personal mission to scour old cemeteries and overgrown burial sites, locating the unmarked graves of long-forgotten people and doing what he can to acknowledge their legacies.

Since 1995, Rieland, who was a Korean War paratrooper, has marked more than 85 veterans' graves with 230-pound marble headstones provided by the federal government and placed 200 homemade aluminum crosses on abandoned burial plots of 19th-century pioneers.

"I read about how hard those early settlers worked, and I thought, an unmarked grave can't be the end of their story," says Rieland, 74, of Delano, Minnesota. "It just didn't seem right to me."

Rieland's mission started years ago while he was paying his respects to family ancestors buried at Delano Public Cemetery. He was puzzled and intrigued by a grave marker bearing the maiden name of his former wife and wondered why the person's full identity wasn't included. He later checked historical records and discovered a 3-year-old girl was buried there.

Another records check of a different headstone revealed that nearby unmarked graves held the remains of two brothers who were Civil War veterans, in addition to two children in their family.

Rieland had read stories about Delano-area men who fought in the Civil War. He marveled at tales of settlers who spent all summer clearing a single acre of land, grubbing out trees with an ax. For brave soldiers and hard-working people of this era to be buried without a trace didn't set right with Rieland.

He began looking up and making copies of old obituaries—10,000 in all—and discovered that many dead were unaccounted for in local cemeteries. He started walking through those grounds looking for clues or slight depressions that might be unmarked gravesites. When he discovered that the federal government provides free markers for every veteran in an unmarked grave, Rieland vowed to do his part to honor them.

For unmarked civilian graves, Rieland makes aluminum crosses and cements each cross into a flowerpot (so it can't be yanked up by pranksters). Then, he digs a hole for the pots at each gravesite.

Having explored and researched many local burial sites, Rieland has gained a reputation as a graveyard sleuth. Now, people from other states seek him out to locate lost graves of family members buried in Wright County and other nearby counties.

One such request came from a woman in Texas looking for her grandparents' graves. "I found them—and 20 other family members she didn't know existed," Rieland says with a smile.

Thanks to Rieland, the Delano Public Cemetery has undergone a needed expansion, and old forgotten burial grounds have been cleaned up.

"Charlie Rieland is now president of the board, and he's the perfect man for that job," noted Allen Swenson, a former member of the cemetery board. "He's got the time for it and really likes what he's doing."

He also is good at soliciting donations from businesses to help maintain the cemetery and places bows on the crosses he's made on Memorial Day, says Neva Adickes, a cemetery board member who has known Rieland since childhood.

Since retiring from the insurance business in 1996, Rieland has worked at cemetery sleuthing nearly full time. Sometimes he finds cemetery records of deaths, then hunts for the burial spot. Other times, he fields phone calls from people telling him of abandoned gravesites they recall seeing as a child.

"Charles Rieland is very dedicated, and when he gets on a project, he's persistent and just keeps going on it," says history buff William Eppel, charter member of the Delano-Franklin Township Area Historical Society. He often turns to Rieland when he's looking for information about deceased Delano residents.

By remembering the forgotten and keeping their legacies alive, Rieland is recognizing the mortality of us all.

"I'd like someone to remember me 100 years from now," he says.

—ALICE M. VOLLMAR

We can each do our part to respect and honor those who have gone before us.

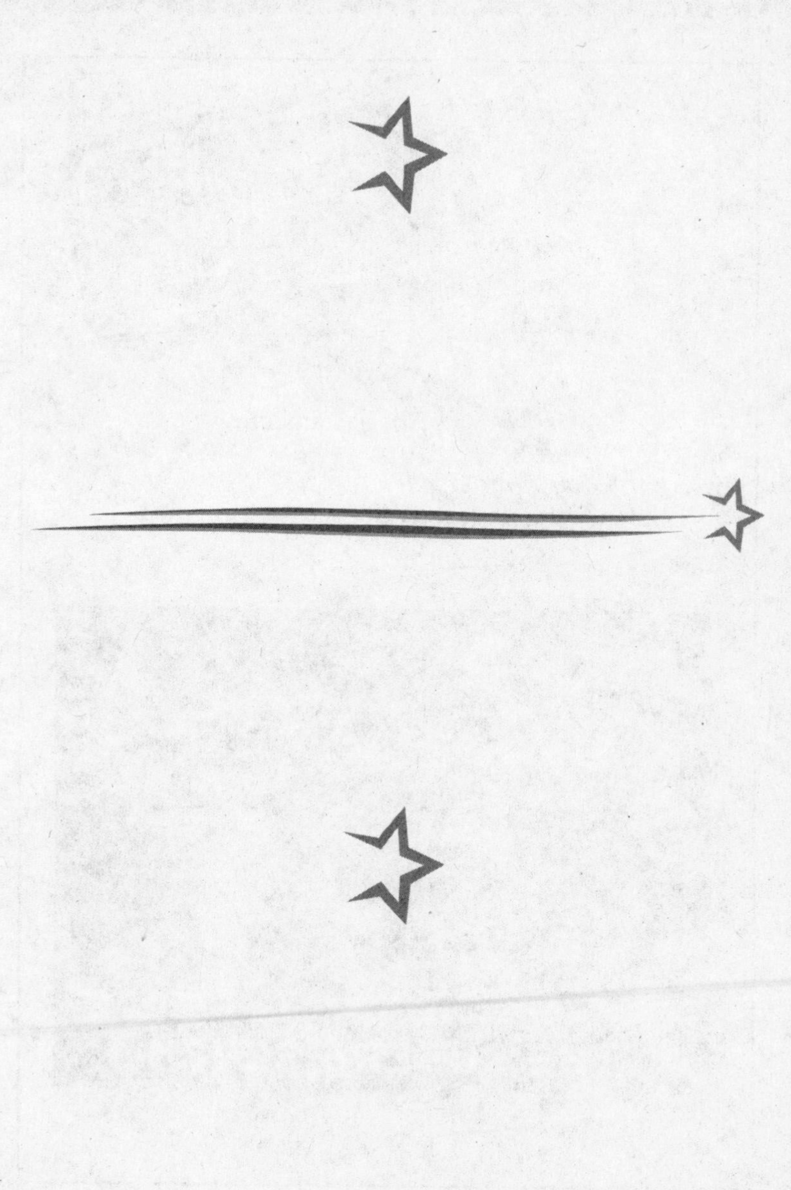

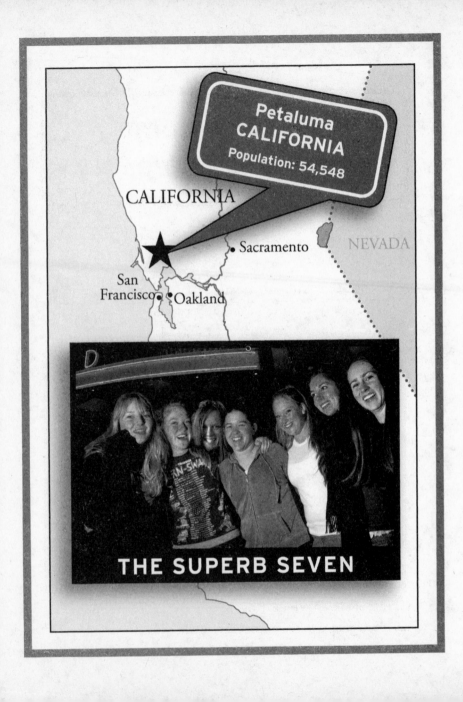

Petaluma
CALIFORNIA
Population: 54,548

CALIFORNIA

Sacramento

NEVADA

San Francisco

Oakland

THE SUPERB SEVEN

Bringing Home the Big Screen

At an age when most girls use their free time to go to the movies, seven teenage girls in Petaluma, California, worked tirelessly to bring the movies to their community.

The teens convinced their city council to build a $9 million multiplex on Petaluma Boulevard in the heart of downtown. But first they had to spend almost four years attending local government meetings, lobbying theater owners and promoting their town as a good place to do business.

Dubbed "The Superb Seven" by their parents, the girls—Noëlle Bisson, 18; Elizabeth Comstock, 17; Ashley Ditmer, 17; Liza Hall, 17; Sarah Marcia, 17; Taylor Norman, 18, and Madison Webb, 17—were the guests of honor when the 12-screen Boulevard Cinemas opened in May 2005.

"We wanted to go to the movies, even if our parents didn't want to drive us," says Liza, now a senior at Petaluma High School. "Our Girl Scout meetings turned into brainstorming sessions. We started talking to people to find out what it would entail."

The need was evident. "Petaluma was the biggest town west of the Mississippi without a movie house," says David Glass, who was mayor at the time. "The girls came to every planning commission and city council meeting and spoke to the issues. It wouldn't have happened without them."

Glass says some interested parties wanted the theater built north of downtown, and he credits the girls for "having the good sense to want it downtown so kids could walk to it." Since its opening, the entertainment spot has infused millions of dollars into the town's economy, attracted new business downtown, and changed the whole flavor of downtown Petaluma in the best possible way.

The success didn't happen overnight. Following a *Business for Dummies* book, the girls developed a master plan for attracting a theater and honed their message as they went. "We were only 11 or 12 when we started, but we came up with most of the plan ourselves," says Elizabeth, who graduates this year from Petaluma High School.

The girls' parents pitched in, driving them to meetings and serving refreshments. The parents and other adults became impressed by the teens' professionalism and grasp of the issues. "I think kids anywhere could be this successful if only one adult would believe in them," says Patty Norman, Taylor's mom.

The Superb Seven divided duties equally and kept one another focused. For presentations before the city council, "we'd all show up at every meeting in business attire, present our business plan, and speak without stuttering," says Sarah, who plans to study marketing and hospitality at college this fall. "People realized we were serious and would do anything to [bring the theater downtown]."

The turning point came in a meeting with Gordon Radley, then president of the California-based moviemaking production powerhouse Lucasfilm Ltd. "I've had presentations by Fortune 100 companies that weren't as professional as those young women," Radley recalls. He became the girls' mentor, introducing them to area theater owners and others who helped fine-tune their business pitch. He also provided a copy of *American Graffiti*, a 1973 film classic that was partly filmed in Petaluma. At a rally they organized to support their cause, the girls projected the movie on the blank back wall of a restaurant—the spot now occupied by Petaluma's new multiplex. "We were nervous before the Lucasfilm meeting," Madison says. "When we realized we'd impressed them, it gave us a lot of confidence."

Their dogged persistence finally paid off. "We were younger then, and probably a bit naive," Elizabeth acknowledges. "We kept going to every meeting and speaking out."

City leaders eventually realized the wisdom of—and widespread support for—a downtown theater. Today, seven plaques honor the girls on the sidewalk outside the multiplex, and five of the seven girls still have part-time jobs at the theater.

"I think [the plaques] are really cool," Sarah says. "We can show them to our kids when we're older. It reminds us that everyone can make a contribution to your community, even if you're only 13 or 14."

—J. Poet

No matter what the goal and what stage of life you're in, it pays to do your homework and to never give up.

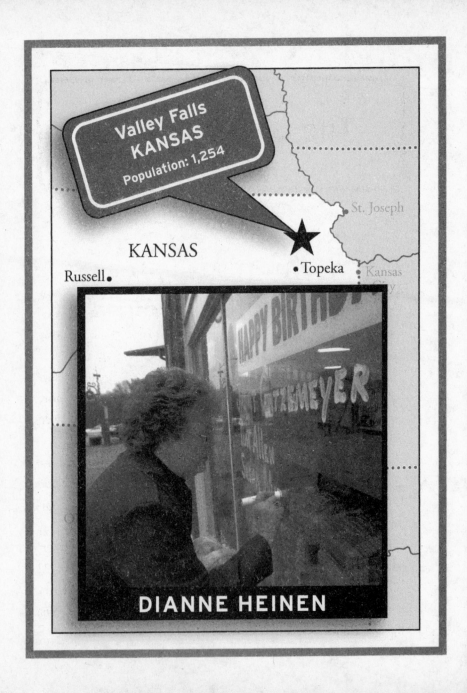

Valley Falls
KANSAS
Population: 1,254

St. Joseph

KANSAS

Topeka

Kansas City

Russell

DIANNE HEINEN

The Birthday Lady

When anyone in Valley Falls, Kansas, has a birthday, everyone knows about it. Every day, 365 days a year, Dianne Heinen writes the names of people celebrating birthdays on the windows of the local feed and seed store.

"It started as a practical joke, just for kicks and giggles," says Heinen, 64, who arrives at the store every morning at 7:30 before heading off to work at her husband's accounting business. Even on weekends, she performs the ritual.

The tradition began on Feb. 22, 1985, when Jim Billings wrote "Happy Big 5–0" on his gas station window to tease friend Patty Brown about reaching the half-century mark. "We were all laughing when she pulled in," he says.

Unbeknownst to Billings, the prank would evolve into a cherished community custom that has continued for more than 22 years. He kept it up for two years whenever anyone wanted a birthday recognized. But when people began making daily requests, that's when his wife, Dorothy, took over.

"People were curious as to what it was all about," she says. "They would slow down and look at the window when going by."

Dorothy maintained the tradition for 10 years, occasionally making a goof, such as a misspelled name. Once, however, she was embarrassed by her inadvertent blunder. "The mortician called to tell me someone I had listed was dead," she says. After that, she was more careful.

When Dorothy became ill, she gave up the daily ritual. "People missed it," she says. "They had come to expect it."

Heinen was among those who noticed the blank window space and wondered why. "I thought it was sad it had ended," she recalls. That's when she volunteered to take over, earning her the title "Birthday Lady" in this northeast Kansas town.

Dorothy turned over her window scrubber, birthday lists, and bucket, with a reminder to Heinen to buy only heavy-duty white shoe polish.

When the list of names grew too long for the window space at Billings's business, Rex Foley, who owned a service station three blocks away, offered to let Heinen use his larger windows. "It took a while for people to realize where it had moved," she says. Foley's later became the Valley Ag building, which sells feed and seed, and where the tradition continues today.

On the windows, Heinen writes the names of local people, as

well as former residents whose names have been requested. Some days she has as many as a dozen names to list, occasionally none. "I still go clean off the windows so it will be ready the next day," she says.

Ordinarily, Heinen doesn't include ages—but there are exceptions. Like the 90-year-old woman whose daughter brought her into town to see her name. "I try to give people like that top billing," she says.

She is especially joyful to celebrate her mother each January 11. The mother and daughter share the same birthday but, at 96, Heinen's mother definitely gets top billing.

"At Christmas, I list Baby Jesus first," she says. To keep it interesting, she also adds George Washington on February 22, Abraham Lincoln on February 12, America on July 4, and, on January 29, Kansas, to mark its statehood anniversary. "That gives a short history lesson," she adds.

One winter it was so cold—11 below zero some mornings—Heinen didn't know if the chilled shoe polish would adhere to the glass. "It was sluggish, but it worked," she says. In the winter, she uses windshield washer fluid to remove the lettering. In summer, just water.

Roy Allen, whose birthday is on Halloween, likes the sense of community embodied in the quaint custom. "I think it is real nice. I look at it every morning," he says.

"It's such a pleasant way to remember people," Brown adds. "My birthday has been up there every year since it began, along with everyone else's in town. It's a wonderful rural custom. It's part of our town."

—Diana West

Take the time to know people by name and know a little about them. That's the beauty of community.

MICHIGAN

ONTARIO

Middlefield
OHIO
Population: 2,233

London

Lake Erie

Portage

Erie

Toledo

INDIANA

Cleveland

Akron

OHIO

WEST
VIRGINIA

BOOKMOBILE LADIES

Delivering Books and a Smile

Edina Szasz sits high in the driver's seat of Geauga County Public Library's bookmobile. She watches the mirrors carefully as she guides the 31-foot-long bus into the narrow driveway of an immaculate Amish farmhouse—one of the bookmobile's weekly stops on its rounds through the countryside of northeast Ohio.

"At first I thought there was no way I could drive this bus," says Szasz, a driver-clerk for the bookmobile since 2001. "But now it's no problem."

Szasz is one of five library workers who steer the rainbow-striped bus out of Middlefield, Ohio, each day to visit Amish communities, senior citizen centers, and daycare facilities, checking out books to patrons along the way. Their mission is to get books into the hands of those who otherwise might not have access.

"We see the same patrons every week," says Sharon Cramer, who has driven the bookmobile for 10 years and hopes to continue the work for years to come. "We really get to know what's going on in their lives."

Cramer and Szasz, as well as the bookmobile's other driver-clerks—Regina Smith, Janet Dickinson, and Cramer's daughter Kim—fulfill a number of roles, including checking books in and out, shelving them, issuing library cards, and keeping the bus moving to the next stop.

"On the bookmobile, we're pages, circulation clerks, reference librarians, and driver-clerks," Cramer says. "Our day goes by so fast. We don't even watch the clock—it just flies by."

At a farmhouse near Parkman, an Amish woman brings her newborn baby out to the bus to introduce her to Cramer and Szasz; at another, Cramer talks with a young mother about the latest novel that TV personality Oprah Winfrey has assigned for her book club.

For both patrons and employees, the bus is more than a library-on-wheels; it's a community center, a reading group, and a circle of friends.

"We try to get our patrons what they need," Cramer says. "We try to think of what they'd like—I'll think, 'Irma likes this, or Mrs. Dettweiler likes that.'"

The bookmobile started rolling back in 1986 with a grant from the state of Ohio. The money went to buy a recreational vehicle, which was filled with books and made a few stops each week.

Demand for the bookmobile's services eventually required a larger vehicle, and in 1992 a bus was purchased to house the touring library. The bus makes 73 stops a week, carries up to 5,000 regularly rotated items—including books, magazines, CDs, and movies—and loans out more than 200,000 items a year.

On order is a new bookmobile bus—with more shelf and head space—to replace the one that has traveled almost 250,000 miles in its 14 years of service. "It will be to us like the Taj Mahal," says Jane Attina, who oversees the bookmobile and the library's outreach services.

For the Amish—who travel by horse and buggy and don't often get to visit Geauga County's public libraries—the bookmobile and the friendly faces of the drivers are especially welcome.

"It's difficult for them to get to the library," says Cramer of the bookmobile's Amish patrons. "Our bus comes to their driveway—it makes it convenient for them. The whole neighborhood will walk down to us."

One such stop is the home of Irma Kurtz and her family. Kurtz and her sister, Amanda Troyer, along with their children, enjoy boarding the bookmobile each week to get a new supply of reading material. "The fact that it comes to my house is a definite plus," says Kurtz, a mother of six. "Our bookmobile ladies are the best."

Driving the bookmobile does have its drawbacks; the bus has no bathroom, for instance, and the driver-clerks have to bring their own bottled water. But these minor inconveniences pale in comparison to the overall experience of driving down country roads, bringing books to people who love to read—and making friends along the way.

"I like this better than just sitting in one place," says Szasz, who moved to the United States from Hungary in 1994. She must speak slowly so bookmobile patrons can understand her lilting accent. "I like to talk to the patrons, and we have a good time," she says.

—VIVIAN WAGNER

Community is born when you reach out and connect with people around you.

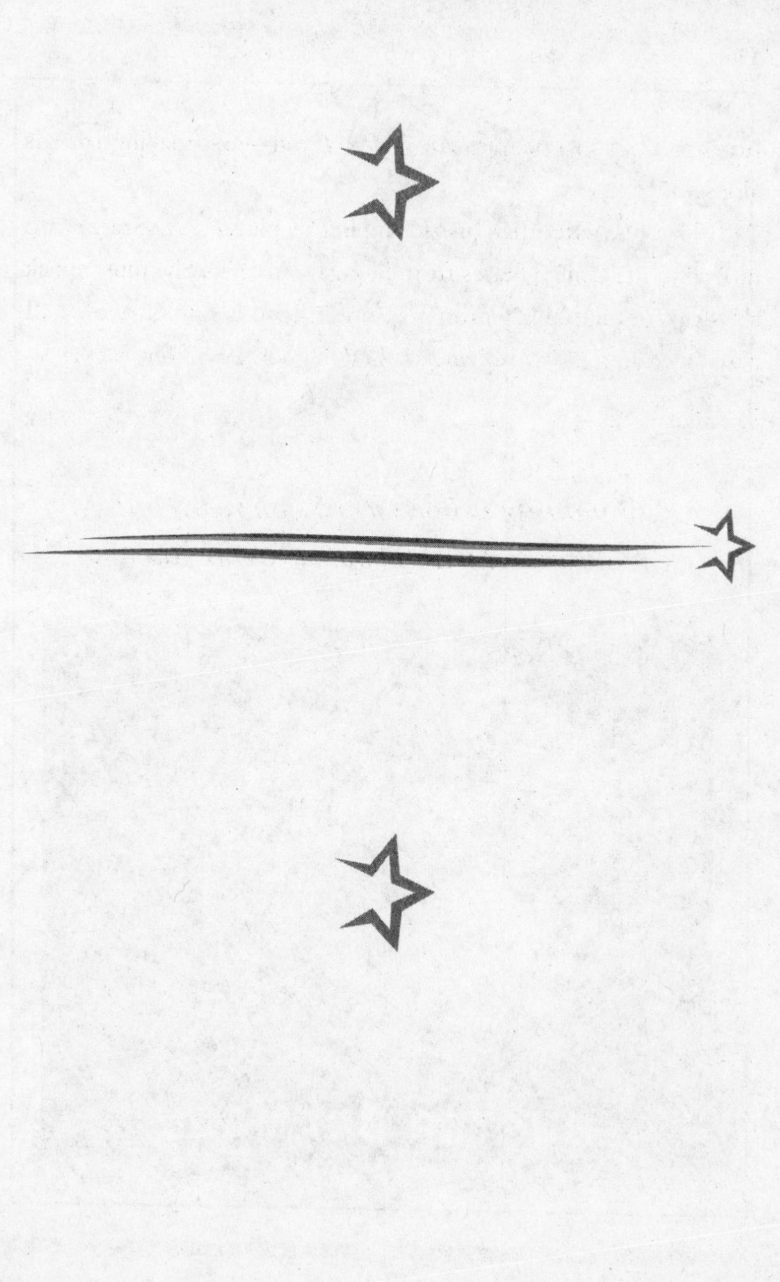

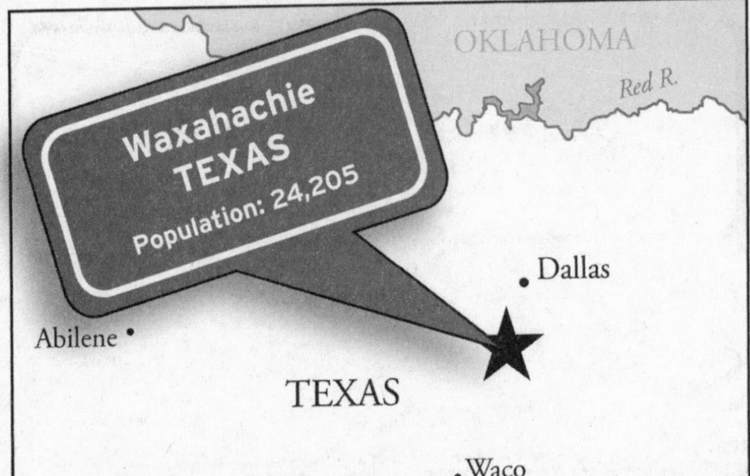

BUSTER BRAMALL

Signing for Santa

Santa Claus sits in a plump, velvet chair in Plano, Texas, while children with gap-toothed grins, excited eyes, and even a few tearful faces line up behind him. The children have never heard Santa's jolly "ho, ho, ho," and many have never sat in his lap to share a Christmas wish list. But this Santa's helper has a surprise. He knows sign language.

"When they notice I can sign, there's a glow that comes over their faces," says Buster Bramall, of Waxahachie, Texas, who has portrayed Santa for hearing impaired children for more than 30 years.

The opportunity for the kids to communicate directly with Santa is what makes the experience so special. In the past, many had to send messages to Santa through siblings or friends. Although Bramall is not hearing impaired, his parents were deaf, so he understands the children's frustrations.

"Before I learned to sign, if my daddy didn't understand something I was trying to tell him, he would say, 'Tell your sister,' (who knew how to sign)," Bramall says. "But I didn't want to tell my sister everything I wanted Daddy to know. It was like going through a third party."

Bramall, now 53, was in his 20s when he began playing Santa Claus for children in a deaf education program in Corsicana, Texas, and five years ago he also began appearing at The Shops at Willow Bend mall in Plano. Between the two locations, about 200 hearing impaired children share their Christmas wishes with Bramall each year.

Speech therapist Sarah Gillette brought a group of 3- and 4-year-olds from the Mesquite Regional Day School for the Deaf to the Plano event in 2005. As each child left Santa's lap, she gave them high-fives and pats on the back. "The kids are used to being in places where people can't communicate with them, so to come here and have someone who can talk to them is really special," she says.

Stella Ashley of Dallas, a long-time friend of Bramall's, plays Mrs. Claus. Like Bramall, she is not hearing impaired, but her parents were deaf and she learned to sign as a child. As Mrs. Claus, she greets the children using sign language and finds out their names and what they want for Christmas, passing along the information to Santa so he can greet each child personally.

Angel Rauls, 7, of Dallas, attends the Dallas Regional Day School for the Deaf and was excited to talk to Santa at the Plano mall. "I asked Santa for roller skates," she says. "If I get them, I'll probably skate with my friends, and I might be able to teach my younger brothers and sisters to skate."

Rauls has a good grasp of sign language, but some children who are just learning to sign bring pictures of the toys they would like. No matter their signing skills, Bramall says communicating with the kids is not difficult, though sometimes their requests can be heartbreaking.

"One girl asked me for a mama and daddy," he says. "It's times like these that I almost lose it and have to breathe deep."

Bramall is a self-proclaimed emotional guy, but Ashley says his enthusiasm, sense of humor, and love of children make him the perfect Santa. Those same qualities have guided Bramall's work for the past 18 years at the Lena Pope Home, an organization in Fort Worth, Texas, that aids struggling families and supports children in foster homes. Bramall is the director of properties and also founded a program that helps 18-year-olds acquire their first vehicle after being released from the foster care system.

Bramall says he "just tries to help out wherever he can," but sharing his creative energy enables him to give priceless gifts to those he meets at work or as Santa.

"As Santa, he's able to bring a certain amount of pleasure to these children, and he is very dedicated to whatever project or commitment he has made," Ashley says. "He's a hoot, and I just love him."

—Kristen Tribe

Listen with your eyes and your heart and you'll be amazed how meaningful the conversation can be for both you and the other person.

Lake Oahe

Mobridge

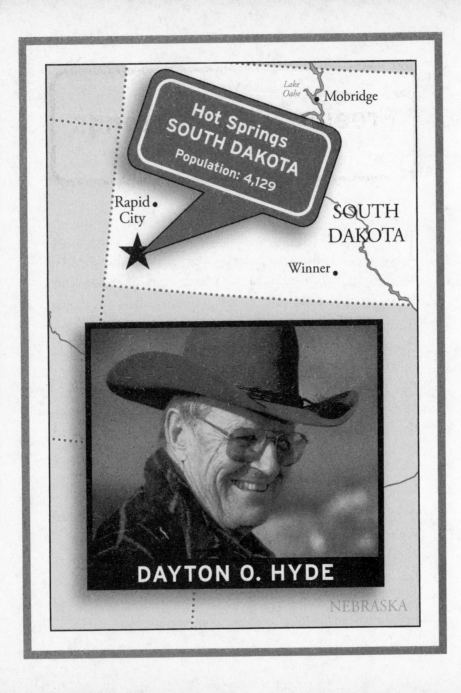

Hot Springs
SOUTH DAKOTA
Population: 4,129

Rapid City

SOUTH DAKOTA

Winner

DAYTON O. HYDE

NEBRASKA

Freeing Wild Mustangs

It's rugged country fit more for beast than man. In the remote South Dakota Badlands, once sacred to American Indians who stalked buffalo on its plains, coyote howls echo off the walls of deep canyons—and 500 wild mustangs run free, thanks to former bronc rider, bullfighter, cattle rancher, and rodeo photographer Dayton O. Hyde.

In the late 1980s, Hyde was driving through Nevada on a trip to buy cattle when he passed a huge government holding pen where wild horses were corralled to protect federal land from excessive grazing. "It made me so mad to see them sad-eyed and dejected that I decided to do something," says Hyde, now 82.

In 1988, Hyde bought an 11,000-acre ranch near Hot Springs, South Dakota, to take in and release captured mustangs. He created the Black Hills Wild Horse Sanctuary to protect not just wild horses and the prairies, but also America's equine heritage.

"These horses represent our Western history," he says, "and it's important to keep this link with the past, to keep this old blood alive. Someday we will want to go back to the mustang to re-infuse their 'smarts' and hardiness into our domestic horses."

To keep the sanctuary's horse population in check, Hyde sells some of the foals each year. Proceeds from the sales and money collected through two-hour guided bus tours support the sanctuary. It is one of the few places in the world where people can see large herds of Appaloosas, paints, palominos, and other wild horses roaming and romping on the open range, watch golden eagles soaring above sandstone cliffs, and witness an age-old American Indian tradition.

Each summer, some 400 Lakota Sioux set up teepees along the Cheyenne River and hold their Sun Dance ceremony, a religious ritual honoring community, courage, and endurance. "I can hear the drumming and chanting clear down in the prairie house where I live," says Hyde, who in 1998 invited the Sioux to convene on his property for the first time.

The sanctuary's scenery is so spectacular that media investor Ted Turner made the 1995 movie *Crazy Horse* on Hyde's property, leaving behind a replica of Fort Robinson built for the production. Disney filmmakers shot scenes of the Wounded Knee massacre for *Hidalgo* at the sanctuary.

Growing up in Marquette, Michigan, far from the Old West, Hyde always was fascinated with horses and ranch life. Eager to become a cowboy, he ran away from home at age 13 to live on his uncle's Oregon cattle ranch in the late 1930s.

He recalls crawling up a rim rock one day as a teen to catch a glimpse of a herd of wild horses that drank from a hidden spring each afternoon. The young Hyde apparently spooked the animals, however, just as an American Indian cowboy was trying to capture several. The Indian befriended Hyde and later left him a gift—two wild foals tied up at his uncle's corral. "They were my first wild horses and I broke them to ride, and my children learned to ride on them," says Hyde.

Impressed by the mustangs' hardiness and intelligence, Hyde learned to catch and break wild horses for ranch work and later took over his uncle's spread. He went on to become a bronc rider, rodeo clown, and rodeo photographer—and a celebrated one at that. Lying flat in the arena and shooting straight up, he captured dramatic, low-angle photos of bucking broncs with all four of their feet off the ground, and often put himself in great danger in pursuit of the perfect image.

"I would get bulls coming over the top of me," recalls Hyde, whose photos appeared in *Life* magazine and later were included in his autobiography, *The Pastures of Beyond,* which detailed his evolution from riding to rodeo, photography, and wild-horse ranching.

Today, Hyde's love of the land and its horses has inspired others. Susan Watt visited the sanctuary in 1995 and has been its volunteer program development director ever since. "I was so impressed with what Dayton had done to protect these horses that I wanted to learn as much as I could from him," says Watt.

Hyde himself has traveled a long way since he was a young cowboy who longed to capture and tame wild horses. Nowadays, all his dreams are about keeping them wild and unfettered.

"I owe these horses for a lot of joy in my life," says Hyde, who has found a way to pay them back. "Now they have a home that can never be developed, where they can race around and be free."

—Karen Karvonen

We can live a full and rich life and leave behind a legacy that honors the ideals we value most by following the adventuresome spirit within each of us.

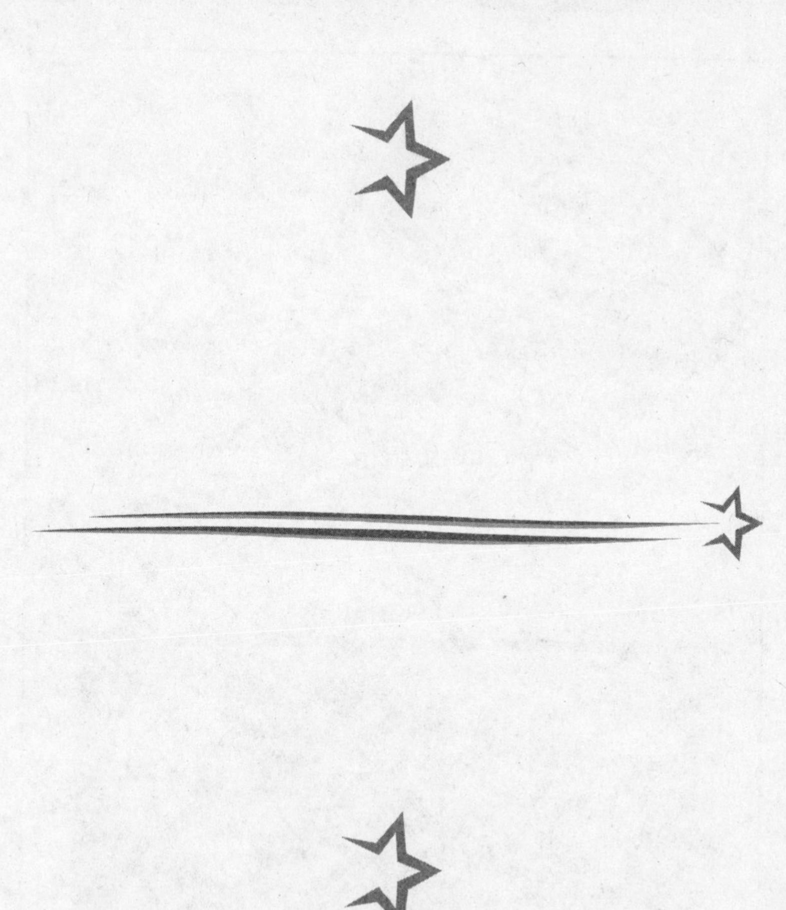

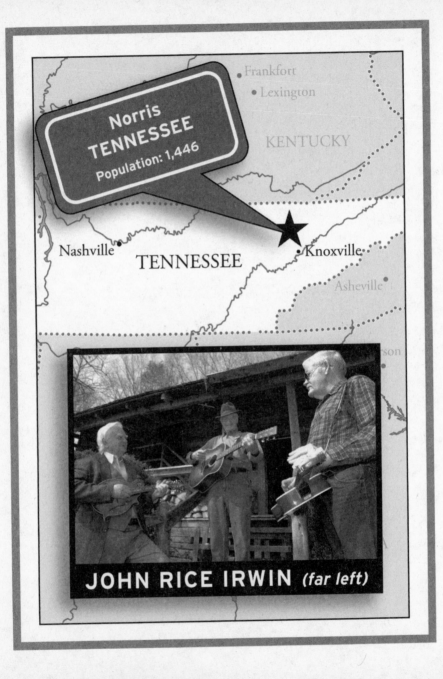

Norris
TENNESSEE
Population: 1,446

Frankfort
Lexington
KENTUCKY
Nashville
TENNESSEE
Knoxville
Asheville

JOHN RICE IRWIN *(far left)*

Preserving Appalachian Treasures

In 1962, John Rice Irwin attended an estate auction near his home in Norris, Tennessee, where he watched as a family's heirlooms were sold piece by piece. One buyer boasted that an old cedar butter churn would make a fine lamp. Another buyer vowed to turn a wagon seat into a coffee table.

Then age 31, Irwin was horrified. He knew the stories behind these artifacts, and he knew how quickly their history was being lost. "Things mean little when they are separated from their history," says Irwin, who developed an early respect for the mountain folk of Southern Appalachia.

So during his time away from working as a school superintendent for Anderson County Schools, Irwin trekked over hills and through hollows buying and preserving relics and the stories behind them. Before long, curious visitors began stopping by his garage to see the items and hear their history.

"When I was little, our garage was filled from floor to ceiling with artifacts he had collected," says Irwin's daughter, Elaine Irwin Meyer, with a laugh. "I didn't know for many years that garages were used for cars."

By the late 1960s, Irwin's garage had reached capacity. That's when he and his wife, Elizabeth, opened the Museum of Appalachia, housed in a log building on a two-acre plot next to his home. Today, the museum attracts more than 100,000 visitors annually and has grown to 65 acres with dozens of authentic log structures and thousands of items—most of them with their stories collected and written down by Irwin, of course.

"When I bought this property, it was just a wasteland of brambles," Irwin says. "Now look at it."

Cattle, horses, mules, goats, sheep, and farm fowl roam the grounds, re-creating an old Appalachian homestead, while musicians often sit on a cabin's front porch singing songs like "Old Joe Clark."

"It was not my intention to develop a cold, formal, lifeless museum," Irwin recalls. "Rather, I aimed for the 'lived-in' look, striving for, above all else, authenticity." That is why, Irwin says, that the Bunch House, the Arnwine Cabin, and other dwellings "appear as though the family had just strolled down to the spring to fetch the daily supply of water."

Most of the rustic structures were saved from demolition and moved from within a 200-mile radius of the museum. The Mark

Twain Family Cabin arrived in 1990 from Possum Trot, Tennessee, where Twain's parents and some of his siblings had lived. "Mark Twain was born five months after the family left here in 1835," says Irwin. The cabin itself was bound for destruction until Irwin saved it. "It was falling down and some of the logs had totally rotted. The owner of the property told me I could have it if I would move it and take care of it."

Irwin had it dismantled and re-assembled at the museum. "It's a shame that so many fascinating and meaningful stories are already gone," he says.

Fortunately, Irwin has saved thousands of stories and artifacts. Take for example, Gol Cooper's glass eye and a penknife on display at the museum. In 1910, young Cooper was tying his shoe and had an opened penknife in his hand. He was stooped over, pulling tight the string when it broke, thrusting the knife blade through his eye.

"Gol's father had an eye made for him and he wore one until he died in 1979," Irwin says. The eye and the knife, along with the story, were given to the museum by Cooper's daughter.

The museum displays miniature carpentry and farming tools carved by Bill Henry of Oak Ridge, Tennessee. A self-taught whittler, he says it's an honor to have his work preserved at the museum. "It's an incredible place," Henry says. "If I would hazard a guess, I would say that 75 percent of what's in that museum would be long gone if it weren't for John Rice. He's a dreamer, but he's a dreamer that makes things come through."

Irwin's passion for preserving history began as a child, listening to the stories told by his grandparents—often as he was helping them with chores such as gardening, gathering maple syrup, and finding pine tree knots for fire starters. "I was very lucky to know all four of my grandparents," he says. "Not a day goes by that I don't think of my grandparents."

As he grew, when he wasn't working or hunting, he frequently visited with old people in the community, and "they taught me a great deal," Irwin says. He found the sons and daughters of Appalachian pioneers to be imaginative, resourceful, gentle, and kind.

Those ancestors often didn't have photographs or recordings, but they passed down their stories and their relics from one generation to another. "When an old person dies, it's like a small library burning," says Irwin, borrowing a quote from his late friend and author Alex Haley, who died in 1992.

The author of *Roots*, Haley visited the Museum of Appalachia in 1982 and became fast friends with Irwin. So impressed was the famous author with what he saw that he built a home across the road from the museum. "The day Alex Haley came to my house, we had soup beans and cornbread," Irwin recalls. "Then he used my phone to call his secretary and said, "I'm moving to Tennessee.'"

Now age 77, Irwin spends as much time as possible at the museum he so loves.

"You hear a lot of people say that they don't like history," Irwin says. "But they do like people and they do like stories. Well, that is history."

—Jackie Sheckler Finch

"We cannot appreciate where we are today, or understand where we are going tomorrow, unless we understand where, as a culture, we've been in the past." —John Rice Irwin

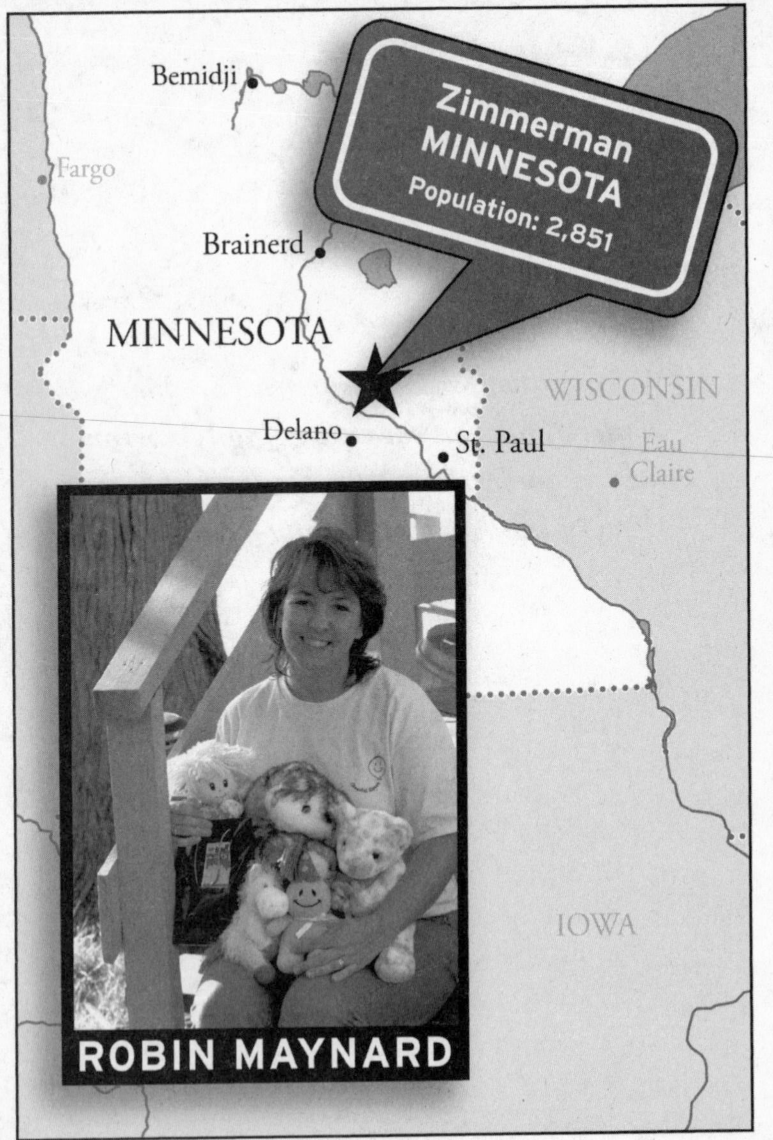
Zimmerman
MINNESOTA
Population: 2,851
Bemidji
Fargo
Brainerd
MINNESOTA
WISCONSIN
Delano
St. Paul
Eau
Claire
IOWA
ROBIN MAYNARD

Spreading Birthday Cheer

In September 1993, Robin Maynard found herself staring at an empty shelf while visiting a friend who ran Trinity Mission, a food bank in St. Paul, Minnesota. Maynard's friend explained that the shelf was meant to stock ingredients for parents to make their children birthday cakes. But more often than not, the shelf held only cans of vegetables or boxes of cereal.

"Can you imagine, it's your own special day, a day that's just all yours, and your parent says, 'Here's some Fruit Loops,'" says Maynard, 40, of Zimmerman, Minnesota.

So she went home that day and told her husband, Kevin, her plan—to buy a dozen bags, fill them with treats, and deliver them to the mission. Maynard dropped off the stuffed "birthday bags" one evening, and by 9 o'clock the next morning, she received a call telling her that all of them had been picked up by needy families.

"They said one mother cried when she saw the birthday bag," Maynard says. "She told the staff she'd changed buses three times to get to the food shelf and had prayed she'd find something she could give as a gift to her child."

From September 1993 to August 1994, the couple bought 1,000 bags and filled them with crayons, coloring books, and toys. Despite their good intentions, the Maynards began to run out of money and could no longer carry the load themselves. In response, Robin started a nonprofit organization called Cheerful Givers.

Today, large corporations donate bags and items such as stuffed animals, coloring books, balls, puzzles, whistles, and candy. The organization is aided throughout Minnesota by more than 3,000 volunteers who buy items themselves, fill the bags, and deliver them to food banks and homeless shelters in Minnesota and Wisconsin.

"The birthday bags of goodies allow us to reach out to children with more than food," says Ralph Olsen Jr., senior pastor at the King of Kings Lutheran Church Food Shelf in Woodbury, Minnesota. "The bags are a sign of love and hope to children who would not otherwise have such gifts."

In 2003, Maynard handed over the day-to-day operations of Cheerful Givers to Karen Kitchel, who now runs the organization from her home in Eagan, Minnesota.

"There are about 110,000 children living in poverty in Minnesota, and that number's rising," says Kitchel, the organization's only paid employee. "I think most charities concentrate on giving children gifts at Christmas, but no one seems to focus on birthdays. We always try to include a lasting item like a stuffed toy in the bags because, for many of these children, it's the first thing they've ever owned."

Kitchel lauds Maynard for finding a way to spread happiness on a child's special day. "The impact Robin has made is incredible. She's a person with a big heart," she says.

Maynard now works in the communications department at Land O'Lakes Inc. in Arden Hills, Minnesota, where she leads a corporate Cheerful Givers team. She has served on the Cheerful Givers board and continues to promote the organization on a volunteer basis.

As of late 2006, Cheerful Givers had provided more than 150,000 birthday bags to children in Minnesota and Wisconsin. And just as Maynard has always done, each bag is given anonymously.

"It's important that the children think their parents are the ones giving them the gift," Maynard says. "Many work two or three jobs just to make ends meet, so they're the real heroes, not us."

—Susan Palmquist

Making a difference doesn't require a million-dollar donation. Sometimes, the gift of a small toy or game can turn a child's birthday into a treasured memory.

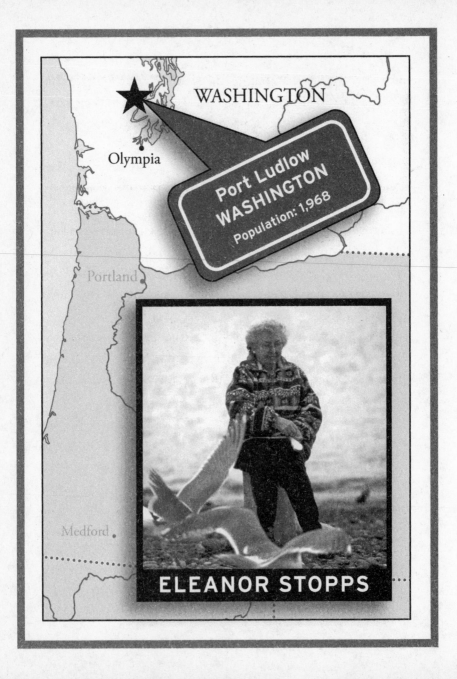

WASHINGTON

Olympia

Port Ludlow
WASHINGTON
Population: 1,968

Portland

Medford

ELEANOR STOPPS

The Bird Lady

Eleanor Stopps's tenaciousness on behalf of wildlife hasn't dwindled a bit since she set out 33 years ago to safeguard her feathered friends on Protection Island. Thanks to Stopps, 87, the island in northwestern Washington—home to 85 bird species—was designated a national wildlife refuge in 1982.

"Even today, if anything goes on, everybody lets me know," says Stopps, who earned the nickname the "Bird Lady" of Mats Mats Bay in Port Ludlow, Washington. "There were problems a few years ago, so I yelled, screamed, and stomped my feet, and it all got corrected," she adds with a laugh.

Her interest in wildlife began in the 1960s while she was a volunteer assistant Girl Scout leader in Seattle. The girls in her troop wanted to earn bird merit badges, so Stopps joined the Seattle Audubon Society to help. Through Audubon, she met artist-ornithologist Zella Schultz and began accompanying her on bird-banding expeditions to Protection Island, at the mouth of Discovery Bay.

Lacking predators, the island had one of the world's largest colonies of rhinoceros auklets (a type of puffin) and the largest glaucous-winged gull colony in the state. It was the only place within Washington's inland waters to find tufted puffins and was a major breeding area for cormorants, bald eagles, and other waterfowl.

When Schultz died in 1974 and island development plans threatened the bird population, Stopps adopted Schultz's mission of protecting Protection Island. The efforts already had led the Nature Conservancy to buy 48 of the island's 400 acres, and Stopps began an intense campaign to save the entire island.

"Seventy-five percent of all Washington birds that nest in inland waters breed on Protection Island," Stopps says. "I felt the only proper use of that land was as a wildlife refuge."

Stopps moved to Mats Mats Bay in the mid-1970s and founded the Jefferson County Admiralty Audubon. Through that, she started the Adopt-a-Seabird program and raised $50,000 to purchase 23 Protection Island lots.

Stopps didn't stop there. By lobbying and letter writing, she gained the support of Jefferson County commissioners, the National Audubon Society, and the federal government. In 1981 and 1982, she testified before congressional committees in Washington, D.C.

After nearly nine years of fighting for her cause, she won a watershed battle on October 15, 1982, when President Ronald Reagan signed the National Wildlife Refuge Bill, forbidding development and human habitation on Protection Island. It was the only national wildlife refuge created during Reagan's eight-year presidency.

"She's one of our heroes," says Peter Badame, formerly of the Port Townsend Marine Science Center. "Eleanor's dedication to preserving irreplaceable habitat is legendary in Jefferson County, as well as within the greater ornithological [birding] community."

Thanks to local organizations and businesses, tourists are able to view the island off shore, where eight mammal species also have been spotted. Once a year, Stopps tries to take part in a tour. "Usually they take me along as a guest and introduce me as a 'living legend,'" she says chuckling.

Stopps has received numerous awards for her achievements, including the Oak Leaf—the Nature Conservancy's top national award—and Citizen Appreciation from the U.S. Fish and Wildlife Service. In 1989, she was nominated Jefferson County Citizen of the Century. She was named a "Giraffe" by the National Giraffe Project, a nonprofit group that honors those who stick their necks out for the common good. And in Port Townsend, the environmental group EarthDay EveryDay has established the Eleanor Stopps Environmental Leadership Award to honor a Jefferson County resident each year who has worked to sustain the environment.

Stopps says she never expected such acknowledgments. "I just wanted Protection Island to be safeguarded for the wildlife," she says. "The birds are as much a part of me as the air I breathe. We're all interconnected."

—CAROLE MARSHALL

It takes only one person to make a world of difference that will affect our planet forever.

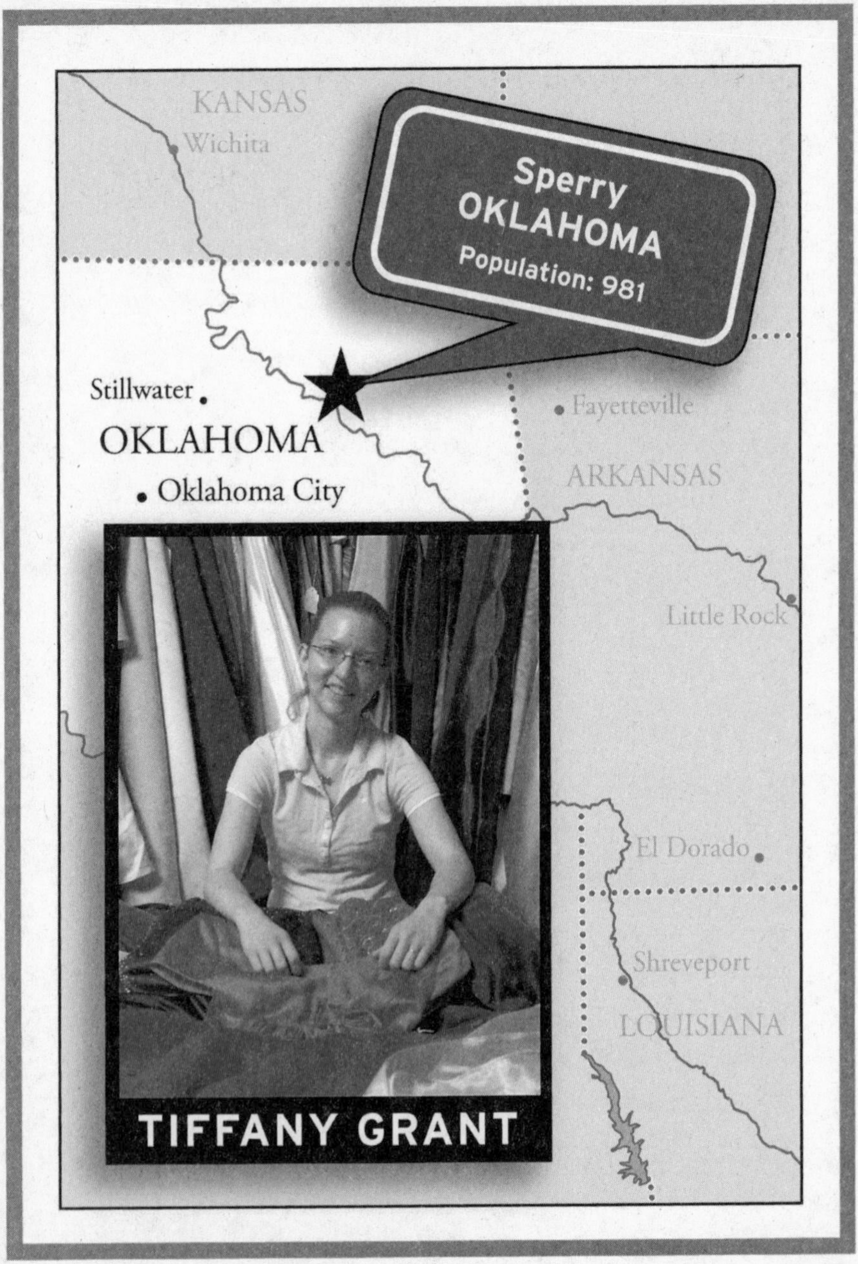

KANSAS
Wichita
Sperry
OKLAHOMA
Population: 981
Stillwater
OKLAHOMA
Oklahoma City
Fayetteville
ARKANSAS
Little Rock
El Dorado
Shreveport
LOUISIANA
TIFFANY GRANT

Granting Prom Wishes

White lights twinkle in the atrium of the CityPlex Towers in Tulsa, Oklahoma, casting a faint glow on her pink satin formal as Tiffany Grant glides across the dance floor with her date. Water cascades from a nearby fountain and a slow country ballad pours through the speakers. The girl from nearby Sperry, Oklahoma, is momentarily swept away by all the pomp and pageantry.

But when a smiling Lauren Bradshaw dances by in a peach dress, the significance of the evening crystallizes for Grant, 18.

"When you see a moment like that, it makes everything worth the effort," says the young founder of Prom Wishes Inc., which provides prom dresses and tuxedos to teenagers who can't afford them. "It's an amazing feeling to see someone have so much fun and know that you helped make the moment special for them."

Last year's prom night was particularly meaningful for Grant, a graduating senior who started Prom Wishes in 2002 as a 4-H project. She began with a few hand-me-down gowns and gave them to

19 girls the first year. Since then, nearly 800 girls and a handful of boys from across Oklahoma have received dresses and tuxedos from the organization.

"This is my passion," Grant says. "I just got hooked from the very beginning. Nobody deserves to stay home from prom because they can't afford to go."

Bradshaw is thankful for the project that outfitted her with formal gowns for her junior and senior years. There would have been no proms for the 2006 Sperry graduate without Grant's help.

"There's no way I could have afforded to go," Bradshaw says. "I would've felt like I missed a big part of my high school years. I'm grateful that I had the opportunity to go."

Prom Wishes does more than provide the dress, however. Like all the other teens, Bradshaw also received jewelry, a matching purse, corsage, and even a boutonniere for her date, plus a $25 gasoline card and gift certificates for a manicure and hairstyle. Individuals donate the dresses and tuxedos while local and area businesses contribute everything else. The formal attire and accessories are stored in a Sunday school classroom at the First Baptist Church of Sperry where prom-bound teenagers can go to pick out their dream outfits.

The stories of people helped are typically poignant. Grant remembers outfitting a girl whose mother died a few weeks prior to prom and her father was laid off from work.

"The dad didn't know what it entailed to get a girl to prom," Grant says. "He had tears in his eyes after we helped his daughter.

If it hadn't been for us, his daughter would have stayed home from prom. He was so grateful for everything."

Fortunately, the legacy of kindness will continue while Grant attends college at Southwest Baptist University in Bolivar, Missouri. After graduating from high school, she handed over the reins to Jamie Weatherman, a seventh-grader and fellow 4-H member who previously volunteered for the organization. Weatherman hopes to double the number of girls served.

"I've got big shoes to fill, but I think this is probably the best thing that ever happened to me," Weatherman says. "Tiffany has shown me that one person can make a difference if they just try."

—Robyn Hoffman

One of life's greatest joys is helping to make a dream come true for someone in need.

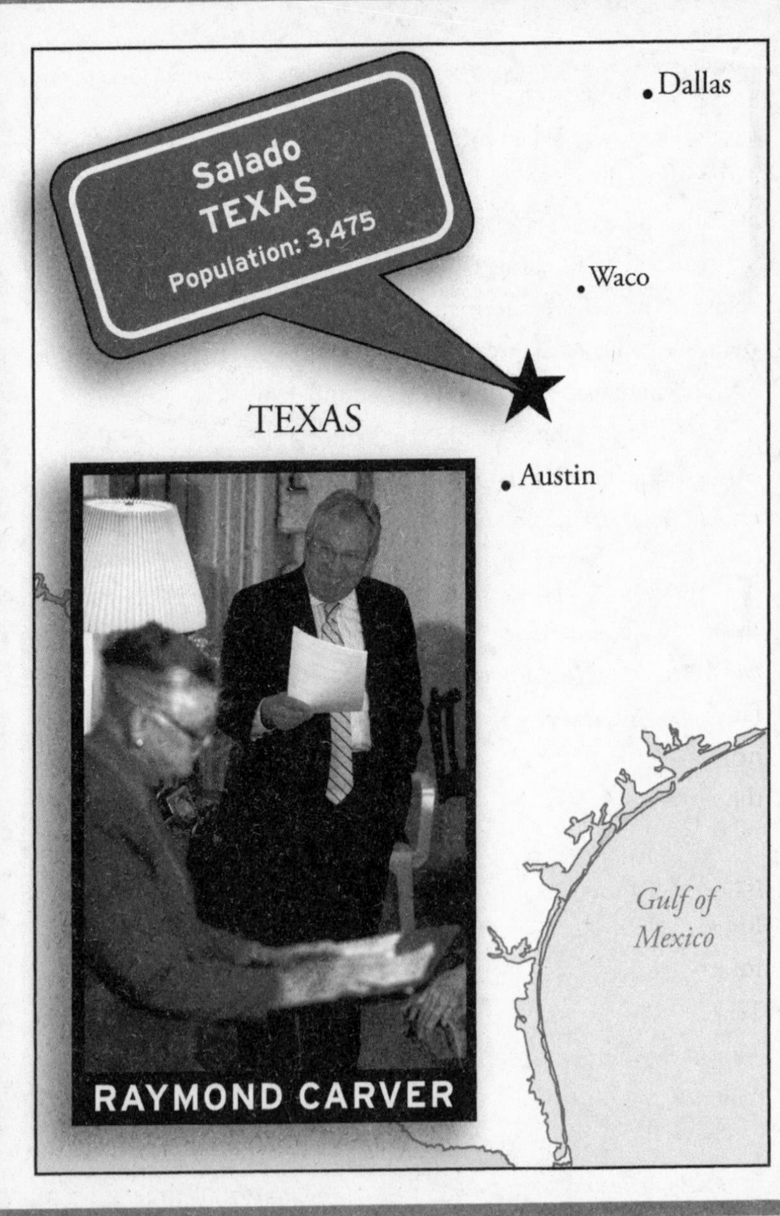
Dallas
Salado
TEXAS
Population: 3,475
Waco
TEXAS
Austin
RAYMOND CARVER
Gulf of
Mexico

Bringing the Theater Home

Dozens of audience members quietly settle into their seats as the theatrical production of *Profiles: Famous (and Infamous) People* gets under way in Salado, Texas. If the actors seem familiar to the eager crowd, it's because the performers are their neighbors. If the cozy surroundings seem inviting, it's because the show is taking place in their neighbor's living room.

Watching the production unfold is Raymond Carver, the mastermind behind the in-home theater company known as the Living Room Theatre of Salado (LRTS). The idea came to Carver, a former drama professor at Angelo State University in San Angelo, Texas, in 1996 when he retired to Salado with his wife, Barbara. Although the town was without a theater venue, Carver was determined to put on a show.

He envisioned an arts group that would bring together neighbors as actors and writers, and productions without the bother of costumes, sets, and lighting. He enlisted the help of the late A. C. Greene, a renowned author, and his wife, Judy. Carver adapted two of Greene's short stories for himself and Judy to act out, and persuaded friends to host productions in their living rooms.

What started out as a one-shot show instead launched the first season of the LRTS, which begins its 11th season in the fall of 2007 with a biographical sketch of a World War II fighter pilot who lives in Salado. Three shows are produced each season, and each production is performed three or four times for a total audience of 125. Tickets are $5, which covers the cost of mailing performance announcements and other production costs. Each performance lasts no longer than 90 minutes and is staged in a different Salado home. Light refreshments are served after the show.

Carver, who describes himself as "ageless at 74," is the theater's energetic producer/director, adapting novel excerpts, memoirs, and other material and recruiting neighbors to read from scripts much like old-time radio actors. In addition to producing adaptations of short stories by Greene, the theater group showcases the works of published and unpublished Texans such as Horton Foote, Elizabeth Forsythe Hailey, and Mike Boren.

The 2005 production of *Profiles: Famous (and Infamous) People* took place in the living room of Paul and Mary Jean Boston. After helping with last-minute buffet preparations, Mary Jean took the stage, where she exhibited her wry sense of humor by reading the part of former Texas governor Miriam "Ma" Ferguson.

The vignettes were adapted from published biographies written by resident Elizabeth Silverthorne, who watched as Salado High School Spanish teacher Barbara Harper took on her first role, portraying Pancho Villa's widow.

"He encouraged me," Harper says of Carver, who coached her for the role. "He has so much to offer. I've seen other people in these shows and marveled at the way he brings out talent in people who have never acted."

Most of the actors have little or no background in theater. They range in age from 6 to 95 and, in real life, include police officers, homemakers, ranchers, teachers, students, and active retirees.

"Raymond has fantastic intuition when it comes to casting," says Charles Barrier, a retired neurosurgeon who portrayed Ashbel Smith, founder of the University of Texas, in the *Profiles* production. The key to the Living Room Theatre's success, Barrier says, includes "the selection of plays, brilliant casting, the social hour, and the feeling of community when people are packed in together."

Carver, who has cast more than 140 people in the shows, says he typecasts and works only with people who are willing to perform. "Everyone has behaviors or characteristics that can work in a particular context," he says.

A few weeks prior to each show, he coaches actors individually on interpretation and timing, then holds a full rehearsal.

Judy Greene, who played a small part in the show, says Carver has a special gift for coaxing realistic performances out of amateurs: "It's Raymond's kindness," she says. "He makes you think you're a star."

—LEANNA SKARNULIS

Use creative outlets to keep your mind agile and your passions fresh, and you will find that others are drawn to you for inspiration.

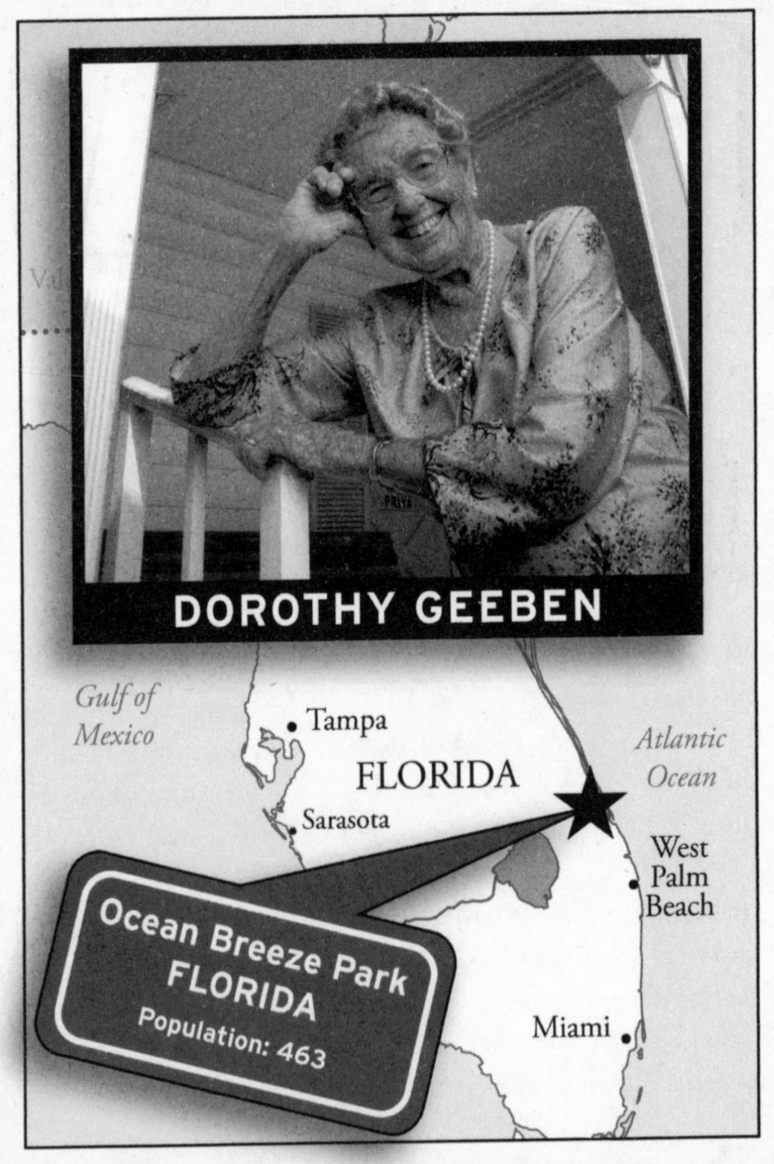
DOROTHY GEEBEN
Gulf of Mexico
Tampa
FLORIDA
Sarasota
Atlantic Ocean
West Palm Beach
Miami
Ocean Breeze Park
FLORIDA
Population: 463

Mayor Dorothy

Dorothy Geeben, the mayor of Ocean Breeze Park, Florida, stands in the entryway of Jensen Beach Christian Church, greeting members and visitors as they arrive for Sunday service.

"Good morning. How are you today?" says Geeben, the church's treasurer and organist, flashing her nonstop grin and hugging friends and neighbors.

It's hard to image that five years ago the little church had no pastor and only four members. Logic called for abandoning it and finding another place to worship, but Geeben refused. Each week she continued to show up, often praying by herself. Eventually, she found a minister and hired him, and the congregation has since grown to about 100 members.

Single-handedly rescuing a church is one example of Geeben's spunk. Being elected mayor that same year is another. And, both accomplishments came as Geeben turned 94.

Now 99, she's believed to be the oldest mayor in the country.

Mayor Dorothy—as everyone in town calls her—moved from Iowa to Ocean Breeze Park with her first husband in 1952. The retirement community, dubbed the "town on wheels" because all residents live in mobile homes, is located along Florida's eastern coast, three miles north of Stuart, Florida.

Twice widowed, Geeben served as president of the town council for 31 years before assuming the mayor's job with the death of her predecessor in 2001. Geeben first ran for mayor in 2002, and was re-elected to two-year terms in 2004 and 2006.

"She's been here so long, she's a permanent fixture," says town Clerk Sharon Chicky. "She had no opposition during every election because everyone's completely happy with her."

Geeben receives no pay, but her mayoral duties are fairly light. She attends monthly town council meetings and signs correspondence and checks. Still, Chicky says, "Dorothy is a bona-fide mayor; it's just that we are very small scale."

"I get complaints, but I just pass them along," explains Geeben, ever the diplomat. Her advice to anyone considering public office is simple: "Like people, listen to them, and be honest in your dealings with them."

"She's a real trooper," says her pastor, Gary Landsberg. "She's very loving and her heart goes out to people."

In September 2004 as Hurricane Frances headed toward Ocean

Breeze Park, Geeben evacuated, then returned to find her home damaged. But, says fellow parishioner Jim Packer, "she had more compassion for others than she worried about herself." And, he adds, "If she's not doing something for the church, she's going here, going there. She's always busy."

"I really don't have much time to sit down and do nothing," says the happy-go-lucky Geeben. "I just wake up and most generally I'm going somewhere so I get up and get going." Geeben teaches a crafts class, plays bingo, and regularly goes out to eat with friends. She does use a walker, but still drives short distances and does her own housekeeping and cooking. She maintains her health by taking her blood pressure medication daily, along with two teaspoons of vinegar and honey.

Geeben has no family nearby, but her son, John, who lives in Marion, Iowa, calls several times a week to keep her up to date on her two grandchildren, seven great-grandchildren, and one great-great grandson.

Needless to say, the elderly mayor has garnered plenty of media attention. Jay Leno called inviting her to appear on *The Tonight Show*, but she declined. "Now that she's famous, I give her a hard time," Landsberg says. "I say, 'You better watch out for the paparazzi.' Of course, she just laughs and takes it in stride."

Taking things in stride is Geeben's credo, and to stay active is the reason she's served all these years. Will she seek re-election in 2008?

Without hesitation she answers, "If I'm alive, so keep your fingers crossed."

—Veda Eddy

You're never too old to be of service to others.

Grove
OKLAHOMA
Population: 5,131

KANSAS
OKLAHOMA
Sperry
Fayetteville
ARKANSAS
Little Rock
LOUISIANA

TYNSY FOSTER

Stitching Bears That Heal

Seamstress Tynsy Foster helps mend grieving hearts with the cuddly keepsakes she creates in her clothing alteration shop in Grove, Oklahoma.

"In 2001, a customer asked me to make a teddy bear out of clothing that belonged to her late husband," says Foster, 58, who since has created more than 1,400 Healing Memory Bears. "Other customers saw the results and the idea took off."

Foster uses her imagination—and a variety of materials—to create the stuffed bears, which become cherished and huggable mementoes of deceased loved ones.

She and her husband, Ron, make the bears for $40 each from almost any clothing material, including suit shirts, sweatshirts, T-shirts, denim, flannel, polo shirts, and robes. "The only materials I can't really work with are sweater material, fur, and leather," Foster says.

Shank button eyes, felt noses, and color-coordinated neck bows give each bear a distinct personality, and Foster's love is evident in the special attention she gives each project.

Sibyl Gines of Salina, Utah, sent an unfinished baby quilt to Foster with the following message: "This was to have been a blanket for a great-grandchild that never came home from the hospital. Can you make a bear, please?"

When Gines received her bear in the mail, it included a small quilt from the leftover fabric. Embroidered on the quilt was the baby's name, birth date, and date of death. Gines surprised her daughter with the bear while the miniature quilt was given to her granddaughter—the baby's mother.

"She could have just thrown that odd scrap away and not done anything with it, but she made a nice little quilt so both of them were able to have something to remember Nicole. It meant a lot to us," Gines says.

Foster's handmade bears have comforted customers from across the nation.

When Barbara Compton, of Bella Vista, Arkansas, lost her husband to lung cancer, she asked Foster to make two bears as keepsakes of the love of her life. "I sent Foster two of my late husband's shirts and had one bear made for myself and one for his 40-year-old daughter," Compton says.

Soon after Compton lost her husband, her mother died. Wanting another bear memento, she sent her mother's mink stole to Foster.

"I knew that if I had it made into a bear it would not be hidden in the closet," Compton says. "I see that bear everyday now and it is a sweet reminder of my mother. My husband's bear sits in the corner of my bedroom so I see it everyday too. They are very special."

Foster's husband helps wherever he can, cutting out the bears for his wife to sew and handling pickup and delivery of packages. The couple says the $40 cost covers materials and shipping costs and that they consider Memory Bears a faith-based ministry. Their gift of love has been returned tenfold. A scrapbook filled with customers' letters attests to the healing power of their cuddly creations.

"Scripture says that we are supposed to grieve for a season," says Foster. "It gives me a sense of peace to know I can be a part of their healing. If you need to cry, you can hug the bear, and talk to it, and have a little piece of that loved one with you."

Before Foster packs a bear for shipping or before an owner comes to claim his animal friend, a special card is attached. It reads, "I'm only a bear. I'm made of clothes from someone so dear who from loving memory will always be here. So when you hug me up close to you . . . just remember that I loved you too."

—Carol Beck-Round

It is a beautiful thing to help the pain of grief give way to the joy of remembrance.

Editor's Note: After Tynsy Foster's story was published by *American Profile* magazine in 2006, the Fosters received more than 1,300 phone inquiries about Healing Memory Bears in the first six months alone. They installed a second phone line and purchased a storage building to house boxes filled with clothing to be made into teddy bears. Ron has cut back on his landscaping business to help his wife. "It is overwhelming to know we can be a part of their healing," says Tynsy Foster.

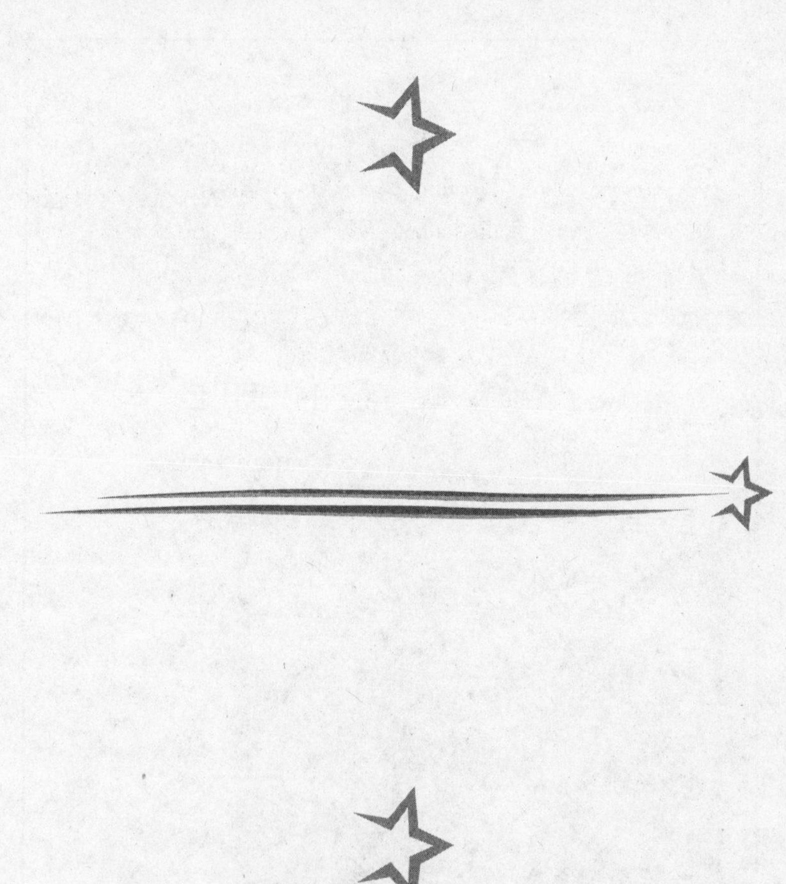

KENTUCKY

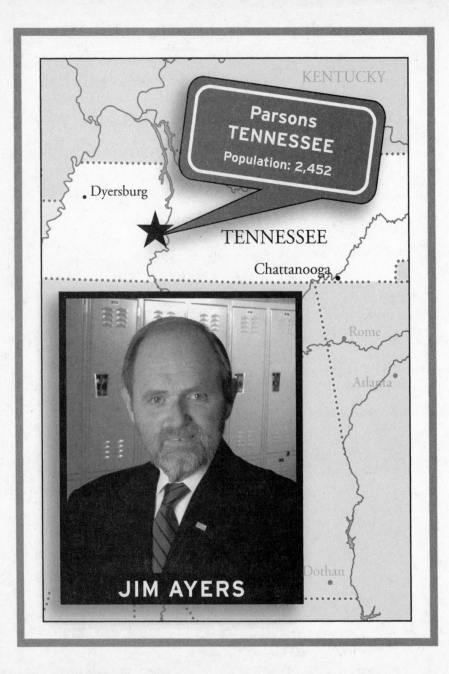

Parsons
TENNESSEE
Population: 2,452

Dyersburg

TENNESSEE

Chattanooga

Rome

Atlanta

Dothan

Sowing Seeds of Success

Jim Ayers isn't a farmer, but the seeds he started sowing in 1999 in the rural Tennessee county he calls home have yielded a crop of remarkable growth.

Through his Ayers Foundation Scholars Program, this self-made millionaire plants the seeds of hope and opportunity for every student who attends school in Decatur County. The foundation makes higher education more accessible to qualifying graduating seniors by granting them as much as $4,000 annually for up to four years. Recipients can use scholarships at any university, community college, or state-run vocational-technical institute in the United States.

The program also provides funding for counseling for seventh- and eighth-grade students and for teachers from three counties to return to school to obtain their master's degrees.

"Education changes lives and communities," says Ayers, 63, who speaks from personal experience. He was born and raised in a modest home that still stands in Parsons, Tennessee, where his father owned a sawmill. Both of his parents attended college, but did not graduate.

"My father never let me work in the mill; that's about the hardest and most dangerous work there is," Ayers says. "From the time I was about 6 years old, there was never any question but that I would go to college."

After graduating from Parsons High School in 1961, he went to Memphis State College to study dentistry. He ended up instead with an accounting degree—and a wife, child, and $8,000 of school-loan debt. Anxious to pay the money back as soon as possible, he took a job as a salesman for Ortho Pharmaceuticals, based in Birmingham, Alabama. His father's death in 1968 brought him back home to Parsons, where he took a comptroller position for a company that operated nursing homes. It was in that industry that he made his fortune, one made larger still by his entry several years ago into the banking business.

"I have been very lucky," Ayers says, sitting in his conservatively furnished office at First Bank on Main Street in Parsons. "There seemed no benefit to me to keep adding up the zeros on my bank statement. I've been to a lot of funerals and I've never seen anyone take it with them."

Instead, he decided to invest in the futures of the young people in his community. But the money, handled and disbursed through the Community Foundation of Middle Tennessee, is just part of the equation. Of equal and perhaps even greater value are the program's administrative and counseling services, which assist students in career exploration, essay writing skills, attending a financial aid workshop, completing a Free Application for Federal Student Aid (FAFSA), and applying for other scholarships.

The program's success is reflected in the numbers. Before the creation of the Ayers Foundation, fewer than 30 percent of Decatur County's high school graduates pursued post-secondary education. Of the 162 young men and women (including special education students) who graduated in 2006 from Riverside and Scotts Hill high schools in Scotts Hill, Tennessee, 136 (nearly 84 percent) planned to continue their education or entered the military. Since 1999, the program has awarded more than $3.1 million in scholarships and helped students obtain nearly $4.9 million in other funding.

Beyond the dollar signs, the students themselves reveal the true value of the program. Jason Rushing was a senior at Riverside High School in 1999 when the opportunity was first announced. He signed on immediately, and went on to earn an education degree in 2004 from the University of Tennessee at Martin and a master's in business administration degree in 2006 from Union University in nearby Jackson, Tennessee.

"You almost run out of words to describe it," says Rushing, now 24 and employed by the University of Tennessee and overseeing a satellite educational program in Parsons. "It just shows you every day what a difference one person can make to an entire community."

—KAY WEST

Invest your resources in people instead of things. Invariably, the return will be greater.

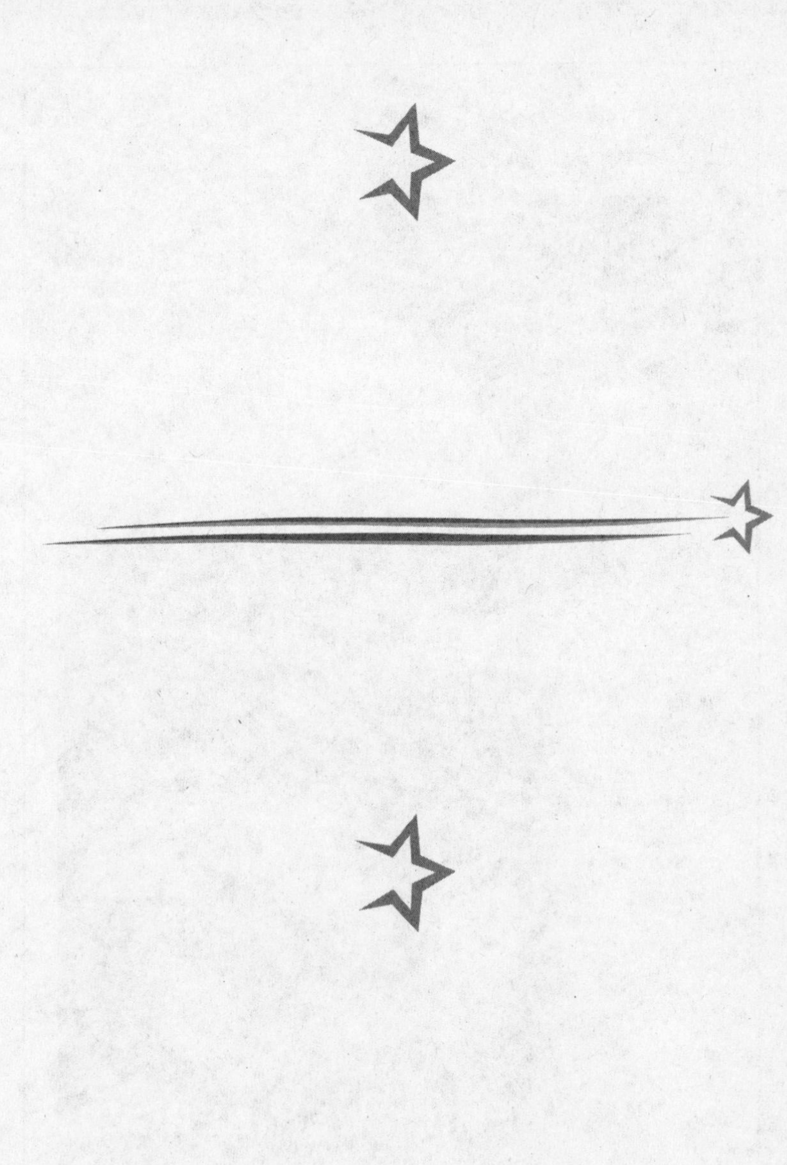

Albany
Boston
MA
Weston
CONNECTICUT
Population: 10,037
Providence
CT
RI
New Haven
NY
NJ
Atlantic Ocean
EMILY WEINBERGER

Orchestrating a Musical Gift

When 13-year-old Emily Weinberger took the stage during a performance with the Greater New Orleans Youth Orchestra (GNOYO) in June 2006, she received a hero's welcome. The young violinist traveled from her home in Weston, Connecticut, not just to perform, but to see firsthand the results of her charitable efforts—a gift of musical instruments, equipment, and more than $2,000 for music lessons.

The idea began in 2005 as Emily's mitzvah (an act of kindness) project, part of the Jewish faith's rite-of-passage into adulthood for girls at age 12.

"Emily told me about her mitzvah project," recalls her violin teacher, Richard Errante. "I had just attended a Norwalk [Conn.] Youth Symphony concert. The audience was asked to give $1 each to help GNOYO in the aftermath of Hurricane Katrina. When Emily heard that, it was as if a light clicked on in her brain."

Music has always been an important part of Emily's life. "I can't imagine living without it and know how hard it must be for kids in New Orleans to be without their music after Hurricane Katrina," she says. So she decided to combine her passion for music with her desire to help others in need.

Using the Internet, Emily contacted Marianna Roll, the youth orchestra's executive director in New Orleans. "Emily explained her project in an e-mail and I responded with a very wishful list," Roll says. The youth orchestra needed instruments, music stands, strings, books, and bows because most of the items were destroyed during the massive flooding caused by the 2005 hurricane.

Emily went to work, devoting her every free moment after school and on weekends for seven months. She called area music stores, which donated music stands, rosin, clarinet reeds, and violin strings. At Weston Middle School, she asked her orchestra teacher if she could set out a box for students to donate musical instruments. She also sent newsletters and e-mails to temple members, friends, and family asking for contributions.

Her appeal was met with enthusiastic support from throughout the community and was "amazing to witness," says her father, Gordon Weinberger. Emily fulfilled and exceeded Roll's original wish list, collecting 27 instruments, loads of musical equipment, and $2,072, enough to provide one year of private lessons to a youth orchestra student in financial need. She even convinced United/ Mayflower Van Lines to ship the items to New Orleans for free.

At Roll's request, Emily penned a letter to the orchestra, whose membership had dwindled from 250 to 125. "I love music and wanted to help your orchestra because I know how much all of you love music," she wrote. "After reading and learning about GNOYO, I realized what a wonderful orchestra it was and wanted to help you get it back to its original state before Hurricane Katrina."

"When I heard Emily's letter, I was so moved," says orchestra member Emily Menard, 16, of New Orleans. "We have the same name and both play the violin. I have friends here without houses, and it was so encouraging to have someone from so far away who didn't even know me to want to do something so touching and loving."

After reading the letter, Roll invited Emily to New Orleans to perform with the orchestra in a summer concert at the New Orleans Center for the Creative Arts. "I love New Orleans, and it was really cool playing with the orchestra I had helped," says Emily, who was presented with a giant "Thank You" card. "Not just adults, but kids kept coming up to tell me that they thought what I'd done was really amazing, and greatly appreciated."

Emily's act of kindness continues to give. "Meeting Emily made our young people realize what an amazing person she is and that she's a kid, too. She makes a difference and so can they," Roll says.

As for the orchestra, membership is growing slowly as displaced families decide whether to return to New Orleans. "Being a nonprofit is always hard, but being a nonprofit after Katrina in New Orleans is extremely hard," Roll says. "Our local sources dried up and it's people like Emily who make such a very big difference."

—Sheryl Kayne

One mitzvah can rejuvenate an entire community.

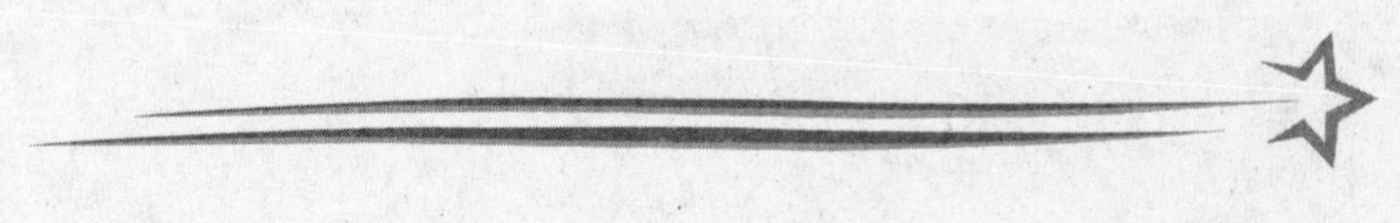

OHIO

Pittsburgh

PENNSYLVANIA

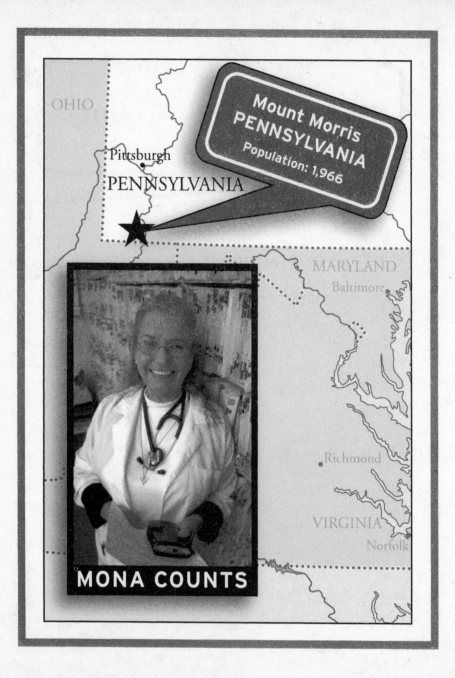

Mount Morris
PENNSYLVANIA
Population: 1,966

MARYLAND

Baltimore

Richmond

VIRGINIA

Norfolk

MONA COUNTS

Knowing What Counts

When nurse practitioner Mona Counts moved to a farm just outside Mount Morris, Pennsylvania, in 1985, it didn't take her long to realize that the people of the impoverished Appalachian region needed better health care.

"People would come in my driveway and say, 'Could you check Johnny's ear? Could you come see my grandma?'" says Counts, 65, who also works as a professor of nursing at Pennsylvania State University.

In the early 1990s, Mount Morris had no medical center and only two part-time doctors—one who came from out of town periodically and one who was preparing to retire. That's when Counts saw an opportunity to offer affordable and accessible health care by employing and training nurse practitioners (NPs).

In 1994, she took out a second mortgage on the 260-acre farm she owns with her husband, John, and used the money to open the Primary Care Center of Mount Morris, a nonprofit health center.

"It was scary, but my husband and I sat and talked about it and thought it would be fine," says Counts of the financial risk. "I thought, 'If you really believe in it, then do it.'"

On its first day, the health center had two patients, including one of Counts's neighbors. To make sure that everyone could afford medical care, she decided to bill patients on a sliding scale based on their income. Thirteen years later, the clinic serves more than 5,000 people from Mount Morris and the surrounding region and averages 25 patients a day.

Part of Counts's mission is to demonstrate that nurse practitioners can provide primary care when a doctor isn't available. Counts and her staff, including four NPs, a medical assistant, a receptionist, a billing clerk, a social worker, and several nursing students, have dedicated themselves to offering the best care possible.

Nurse practitioners focus on providing preventive health care, but they also can diagnose illnesses, order some medical tests, and prescribe certain medications. Many Penn State students work at the center, and Counts encourages them to establish similar clinics someday in other rural areas.

"Mona is such a neat person to work with," says Lori Blackwell, the center's CEO. "I've learned a tremendous amount from her. She's a pioneer in everything she does."

Local residents have responded favorably to the clinic, in part because of Counts's open and understanding attitude toward the Appalachian people she serves. To her patients, she's not an outsider, even though she grew up in Miami.

"They wanted someone who understood the culture and didn't talk down to them," says Counts, who wants someday to build a 10,000-square-foot, full-service wellness center, including a pharmacy and optometry office. "They were all excited that they had someplace close that would help them, that would listen."

In return, patients remain fiercely loyal to the health center, its employees, and Counts. Jeannie Russell, a Mount Morris resident who chairs the center's board, echoes the sentiments of many other patients. "They're always there when you need them," Russell says. "They work with you as a patient, not as a number or a case file."

The center's employees have a similar sense of loyalty, both to the clinic and to Counts. "Everyone loves Mona," says Rhonda Snyder, a nurse at the clinic since 2004. "I think Mona is just amazing. What she's done is incredible."

—Vivian Wagner

If you take a risk to help other people, the gamble usually pays off.

• Bakersfield

CALIFORNIA

• Ojai

• Los Angeles

• Palm Springs

Las Vegas

Pacific Ocean

Aliso Viejo
CALIFORNIA
Population: 40,166

PASTOR DENNY BELLESI

Pay It Forward

"Dream with me," Pastor Denny Bellesi asked members of his church's Missions Outreach team. And they did, giving him $10,000 in church funds and the go-ahead for an unorthodox project that would reach far beyond one pastor and one parish.

The year was 2000, and Bellesi, founding pastor of Coast Hills Community Church in Aliso Viejo, California, had just watched *Pay It Forward*, a movie about a boy challenged by a teacher to change the world—or, at least, to change his little corner of the world. "I was about to begin a series on stewardship," he says. "The timing was perfect."

That November, Bellesi asked for volunteers and handed out $100 each to 100 members of his church. Referring to the biblical parable of the talents in Matthew 25, he told them, "You must use this money to further God's kingdom, and you must give an accounting and report in 90 days." Through a project designated "The Kingdom Assignment," parishioners applied their talents and turned the $10,000 into more than $500,000—and helped scores of people in the process.

Parishioner Terry Zwick matched the $100 with $100 of her own money and asked friends celebrating a birthday at a restaurant to do the same. When she left the party, Zwick not only had $1,800, but also the name of a woman in need of financial help. Zwick helped the woman pay her rent and purchase Christmas gifts for her children.

Zwick then went beyond the initial project by overseeing the development of Hope's House, a shelter that helps people get back on their feet following family hardships. "From all the positive attention and great excitement from the Kingdom Assignment, it gave me an already prepared platform to share our dream for a women and children's shelter," she says.

When Bellesi called for a second Kingdom Assignment, in 2001, he invited parishioners to sell something and bring the money to church, a project that raised $120,000 for Orange County's poor.

Church members Lou and Tamara Spampinato sold clothing, lamps, and a dresser. "It's enabled my husband and me to really use this as a teaching experience for our two children as well," Tamara says.

For the third Kingdom Assignment, in 2002, Bellesi asked his parishioners to offer their time—to give 90 minutes in 90 days to someone the Scripture refers to as "the least of these."

"Giving doesn't take a lot of money," says Zwick. "All it takes is compassion for someone in need."

Bellesi believes remarkable things happen when compassion is unleashed in a hurting world. "When people work together," he says, "they are building upon a combination of gifts and talents that opens the floodgates for more results, if and when they work together and in cooperation to accomplish a common purpose."

The pastor left Coast Hills Community Church in 2004 but continues to speak to retreats, conferences, and other churches about the beauty of paying it forward. Bellesis and his wife, Leesa, have written three books—*The Kingdom Assignment*, *The Kingdom Assignment 2,* and *The Kingdom Assignment 3*—based on some of the experiences at Coast Hills.

"With the books, we've gotten people all over the world doing Kingdom Assignments," says Leesa. "It seems to be a living organism that has a life of its own that God decides to use when he wants."

—CAROLE MARSHALL

You never know the impact you can have with a little inspiration and a lot of faith.

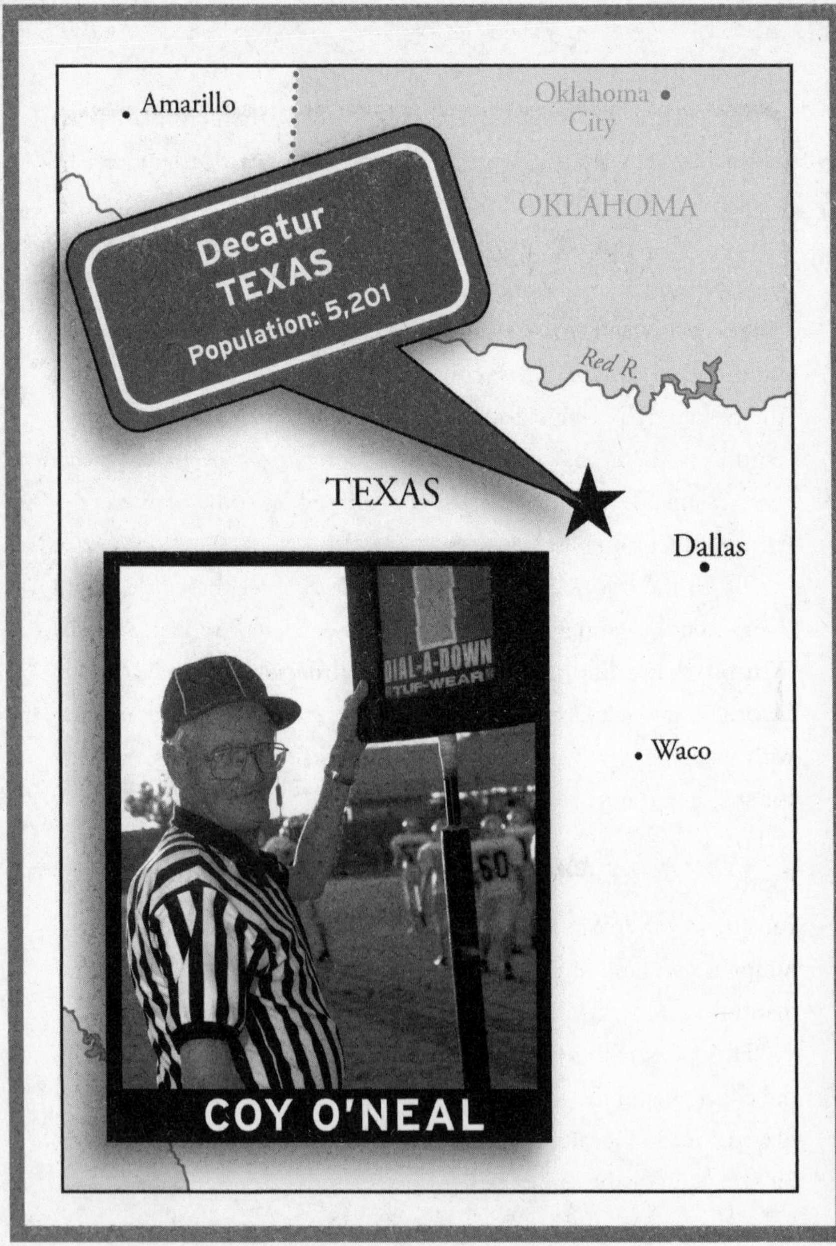

Amarillo

Oklahoma City

OKLAHOMA

Decatur
TEXAS
Population: 5,201

Red R.

TEXAS

Dallas

Waco

DIAL-A-DOWN
TUF-WEAR

COY O'NEAL

Standing Tall on the Sidelines

In football, some men are famous for remarkable speed, while others are recognized for their brute strength or the finesse with which they throw the ball. Coy O'Neal, however, is famous for standing on the sidelines.

For 58 years, O'Neal has been a sideline official for the Eagles football teams in Decatur, Texas. As part of the chain crew, he runs the down marker at all home football games, including varsity, junior varsity, and middle school. At age 74, he's a Decatur Eagles institution.

"He's as much a part of the football team as the quarterback, the coaches, and the fans," says Stephen Wren, a longtime fan who played for the Decatur Eagles in the mid-1960s and then watched his son play for the same team 30 years later.

Greeted at the stadium by slaps on the back and handshakes, O'Neal is well known. His wiry, 6-foot–2-inch frame makes him easily recognizable, and conversation often leaves little time for a concession stand hot dog dinner.

O'Neal couldn't have imagined his future notoriety when, as a teenager, he was pulled from the stands at an away game to help a short-handed chain crew. He says he's "just done it ever since," and since 1948, he's missed only six home games.

"Football is one of my favorite sports, and I just enjoy being on the sidelines," O'Neal says. "Plus, just about the whole town comes to the games, so I get to see a lot of people I know."

"I see him almost every night of the week during football season," says head coach Kyle Story. "Coy's always here supporting the team. He's got a huge heart, and he's someone who really cares about the kids."

On game nights, the high school band blares the Decatur fight song as players take the field. Coaches shout excitedly, straining to be heard over the cheering crowd, and in the midst of the mayhem stands O'Neal, feet planted shoulder-width apart, with one hand on the pole and the other on his hip. He usually walks slowly, but when it's time to move the chains, he summons the energy for a stiff-legged trot.

As an official, he is not allowed to cheer for the team, and while he tries his best, there have been times he couldn't help himself. In the 1960s, O'Neal had a rabbit's foot that he rubbed for luck, recalls Gary Prescott, a former coach who played on the team at the time. During a district championship game, the score was tied, and the Eagles were driving down the field in the final minutes. O'Neal was rubbing that rabbit's foot after every play and quietly chanting, "Go, Decatur, go!" Prescott says.

O'Neal graduated from Decatur High School in 1954 and played football one year—not long enough to earn a treasured letter jacket. In the decades since, the team has given him six letter jackets in honor of his loyalty, which he proudly wears. Three are worn out, he says.

The spirit of dedication comes naturally to O'Neal, a warm-hearted man who has devoted himself to the three most significant parts of his life: his wife, Laverne, who died in 2003, his work at the Decatur Church of Christ, and football.

"He's a special person," Prescott says. "We worry about him now at his age, but who could ever take [his sideline post] away from him? He loves it so dearly."

O'Neal says he's been knocked down only six times, and little do the fans know, but he's got a plan. "I'd like to do it two more years," he says, which would bring his total years of service to 60.

His niece fully expects O'Neal to reach that goal. "He and my Aunt Laverne were two of the greatest fans of the Decatur Eagles that I've ever seen in my life," says Roxie Gernand of Montgomery, Texas. "This fulfills his vision of helping people. I think the young people are really important to him, and he wants to help other people see their own potential."

As fans file out of the stadium and the lights go out, O'Neal finds himself surrounded once again, sometimes by friends or players thanking him just for being there. Humble and unassuming, he usually doesn't have much to say. He brings a quiet spirit to the sidelines though, and the fans consider him a shining star in the Friday night lights of Decatur.

—KRISTEN TRIBE

Whether your position is at midfield or on the sidelines, fill it with fierce commitment and dedication.

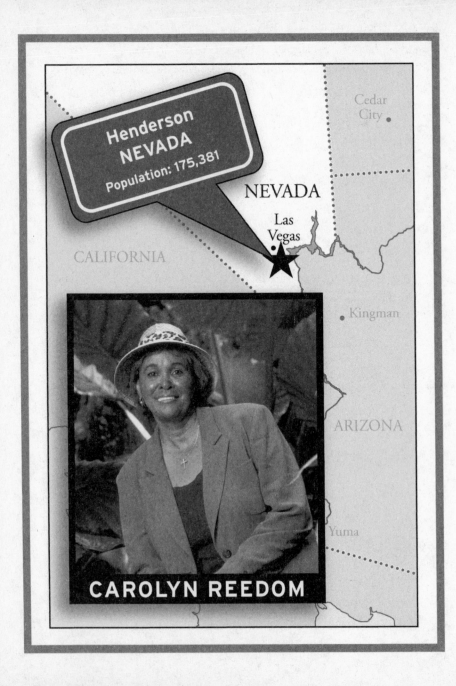

Henderson
NEVADA
Population: 175,381
Cedar City
NEVADA
Las Vegas
CALIFORNIA
Kingman
ARIZONA
Yuma
CAROLYN REEDOM

Raising a Rainforest

When Carolyn Reedom became the principal of John C. Vanderburg Elementary School in Henderson, Nevada, in 1996, she was determined to excite the school's students and teachers about science.

"Science is a difficult subject to teach," says Reedom, who spearheaded the building of a marine lab when she previously served as principal at Estes McDoniel Elementary School in Henderson. "I wanted to do something similar by providing a lab where kids could study, work, and develop a strong science background."

She had plenty of ideas. But at the top of her wish list was building an onsite 3,000-square-foot rainforest biosphere containing hundreds of plants and animals. Of course, the idea of a rainforest in a city located in the desert sounded bizarre to many.

When she first mentioned the ambitious project to the school's teachers, silence filled the room, recalls Joyce Schneider, a third-grade teacher at Vanderburg. "We thought, 'Wow, this is big,'" she says. "But we also knew that when Dr. Reedom decided to do something, there was a way to make it happen."

Getting support from faculty was easy, but Reedom knew that paying for such a project would be a massive undertaking. "We couldn't raise $1 million selling cookies and candy," Reedom says. "If this was something we wanted to do, the community had to help us."

She sent letters to students' parents, introducing herself and her rainforest idea. She wasn't sure how they'd react, but slowly, excitement started building. Parents began mailing cash contributions and donating services, everything from carpentry to plumbing. Reedom wrote a proposal and received a $150,000 federal grant to train teachers about rainforests. She formed a community task force to coordinate project details and fund-raising events such as the Run for the Rainforest 5K run and one-mile walk.

Back at school, she created "DEER Day," an acronym for "Drop Everything Else and Research." For six months, students spent one hour a week learning about rainforests and occasionally met with local architects to exchange design ideas.

After several years of planning and dreaming, Reedom was elated and a bit relieved when ground was broken for the rainforest in 1999. But not everything proceeded smoothly. "It was frustrating when contractors who volunteered their time didn't show up for work," she says. "We had to start all over again and find someone to do their work. It took a lot of persistence and perseverance, but I never felt like giving up."

By the time the rainforest opened in 2002, more than 200 people had worked on the $1.4 million project. The community contributed $250,000 in cash, and more than 70 companies donated labor and supplies.

"We did it!" says Reedom, who was promoted to assistant superintendent of the school district's southeast region in 2001. "And it was far greater than what I had envisioned."

The 3,200-square-foot rainforest is inhabited by more than 100 species of plant life, a 5-foot-long iguana called Iggy, two cockatoos named Ben and Angel, a macaw, two geckos, turtles, tree frogs, red-spotted chameleons, and dozens of finches that fly free in the biosphere. A Mayan temple with authentic rainforest artifacts sits inside the front entrance. Other features include a computer lab, an amphitheater for storytelling, a waterfall and pond, sand boxes used to simulate archeological digs, and a laboratory for growing plants. The rainforest's first snake—a Brazilian rainbow boa constrictor—is on order.

The project's annual $140,000 maintenance fees are funded by the John C. Vanderburg Rainforest Biosphere Foundation, says Catherine Maggiore, the elementary school's current principal. "Dr. Reedom's ability to make science come alive for students is greatly appreciated by everyone," says Maggiore, adding that Reedom has earned a reputation for achieving the impossible.

Because the rainforest is a fieldtrip destination for Nevada school children—with an average of 60 groups visiting each year—parents and students are trained as tour guides. Elizabeth

Kahan was 10 when she served as a guide in 2004 and says the experience boosted her self-confidence and her science grades to straight A's.

"The rainforest is a very cool idea," Elizabeth says. "My favorite part is the animals. I love to help animals and to save stuff like plants, which are homes for many animals."

A favorite part for parents and teachers has been seeing test scores rise over the past five years. The rainforest is credited with helping increase science proficiency among the school's 800 students from 75 percent to 88 percent based on the Nevada Criterion Referenced test.

Looking back, Reedom is proud of what everyone accomplished, and vice versa. The school district has announced plans to name a new elementary school after her when it opens in 2008.

"Our kids deserve whatever we can give them and more," says Reedom, now retired from the school district and working as an educational consultant. "I knew this was going to be a great way to get kids turned on about science."

—CAROL PATTON

Don't be afraid to dream. Good ideas can become a reality with optimism, enthusiasm, and the help of those who catch your vision.

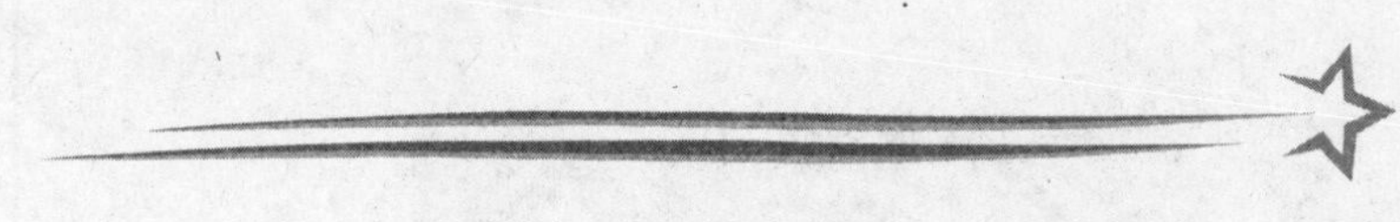

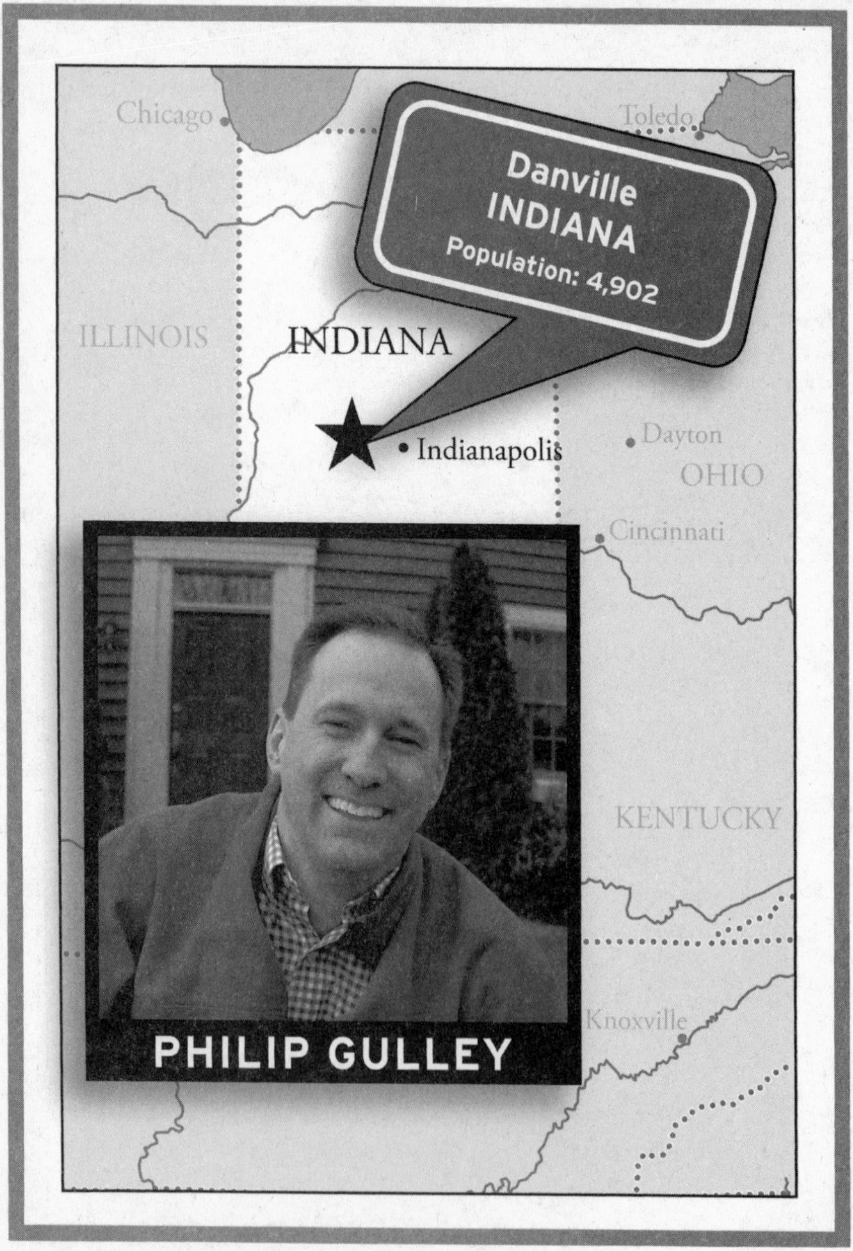

Chicago

Toledo

Danville
INDIANA
Population: 4,902

ILLINOIS

INDIANA

Indianapolis

Dayton

OHIO

Cincinnati

KENTUCKY

Knoxville

PHILIP GULLEY

Hometown Humorist

Philip Gulley never set out to be a writer. In fact, he got a D in English composition in college. "I passed the course with a D only because I promised my professor I would never write again," Gulley admits.

Years later as a Quaker minister, however, Gulley began writing short essays for his church bulletin. Through a happy twist of fate, the essays were passed along to famed radio broadcaster Paul Harvey, whose son visited Gulley's church in Indianapolis. The national radio commentator was later placed on the newsletter mailing list and spread the "rest of the story" of the writing pastor, changing Gulley's life forever.

Now the 46-year-old writer from Danville, Indiana, has devoted readers who have fallen in love with his make-believe Harmony, a charming small town whose poignant stories and folksy characters are recounted in a half dozen books published since 1997. His titles include *Front Porch Tales, Home Town Tales, Home to Harmony, Just Shy of Harmony, Christmas in Harmony, Signs and Wonders: A Harmony Novel,* and *Almost Friends.*

"I get a lot of letters from people who say, 'I grew up in the town you write about and wish I could live there again,'" says Gulley, who has been called Indiana's Garrison Keillor. "The town of Harmony seems so real to me that I feel like I can walk down the street and see the people I write about. It's hard for me to think of them as fictional characters. I keep expecting to see them any day now."

Divine inspiration gave him the name for his imaginary town. "I was reading one day in the Bible and came across the verse, 'I desire therefore that you live in harmony with one another.' That seemed like such a good name for a place like where I grew up."

Gulley grew up in Danville, the fourth of five children in a strong Catholic family. He became a Quaker as a teenager when neighbors invited him to attend their Quaker church youth group. Now pastor of Fairfield Friends Meeting in Camby, Indiana, Gulley and his wife, Joan, are raising two teenage sons.

"I enjoy making people laugh," Gulley says. "I want people not to take themselves and their religion so seriously. Bad things start happening when people take themselves and religion too seriously."

Drawing on composites of people he has known, Gulley has created unforgettable Harmony characters such as minister and book narrator Sam Gardner. Like Gulley, Sam returns to his hometown when he is offered a job after the town's Quaker pastor dies in an accident. "Both his parents had died of heart problems, which he feared would happen to him, so he'd begun to jog and was hit by a truck."

Then there's Miriam Hodge, head elder of the town's Quaker meeting. "She is patterned after a lady in my first church," Gulley says. With a heart of gold, Miriam nevertheless finds herself in some embarrassing situations. In one tale, the ladies of the Quaker meeting decide to make a quilt as a fund-raising project. All goes well until they hang the quilt in the meetinghouse and the sun hits it. Suddenly, the face of Jesus appears on the illuminated quilt. Folks begin flocking to see the holy fabric and Miriam knows she must confess a secret to her minister—she spilled coffee on the quilt, creating a stain that resembles the face of Jesus. "That's not the Lord we've been seeing," Miriam admits. "That's Maxwell House."

Readers sometimes ask how Gulley comes up with the names of his characters. "They are real names," Gulley acknowledges. "The Quakers have a directory of members so I just open it up, put my finger on one name for a last name. Then I skip a few pages and put my finger on a name for a first name."

Gulley's own life is often an inspiration for many of the happenings in Harmony. In his newest novel, *Almost Friends*, pastor Sam takes a leave of absence from Harmony Friends Meeting House, and the church quickly becomes enamored of his temporary replacement, a female pastor named Krista Riley. "I did take a sabbatical last summer for three months and they hired a woman for while I was gone," Gulley says. "When I came back, they asked if I wanted to take another month off."

Sometimes, Gulley's parishioners joke about being fodder for his stories. "We were having new toilets put in our restrooms recently and there was a discussion over whether they should be round or oval," he says. "After about a half hour, I just started laughing and they realized how preposterous it was. They started laughing and said, 'You'd better not write about that in your book.'"

In the end, all seems to turn out right in Harmony. "People always think small towns are boring," Gulley says. "But to me, small towns are fascinating. You can find opportunities for relationships in a small town unlike anyplace else on Earth."

—Jackie Sheckler Finch

Be grateful that God has a good sense of humor.

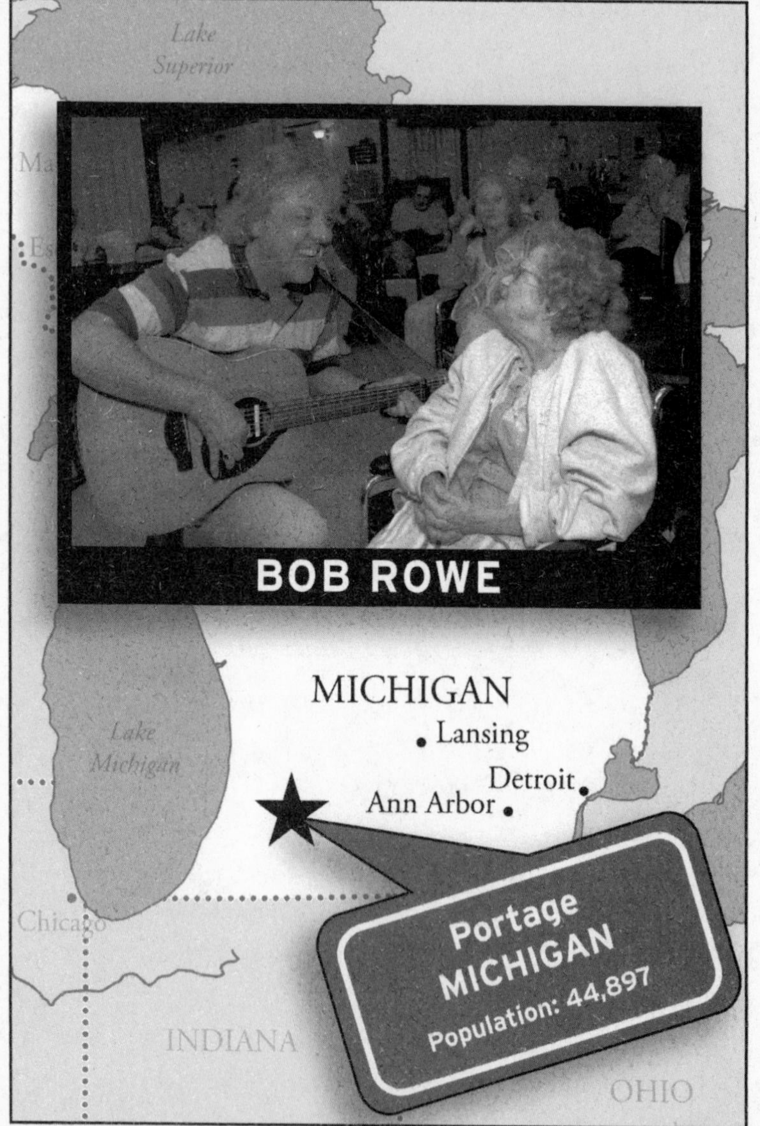
Lake
Superior
BOB ROWE
MICHIGAN
Lansing
Detroit
Ann Arbor
Lake
Michigan
Chicago
Portage
MICHIGAN
Population: 44,897
INDIANA
OHIO

Making Music with a Mission

Bob Rowe bursts into a chorus of "This Little Light of Mine," and residents at the Grayling Nursing & Rehabilitation Community in Grayling, Michigan, tap their toes and sing along—except for one woman, who slumps dejectedly in her wheelchair.

"I went over, kneeled down, looked right into her face, and sang just to her," Rowe recalls later. "She lifted up her head really slowly, gave me the biggest wink you ever saw, and grinned. Then she straightened up in her chair and started clapping and singing."

Such transformations are nothing new to Rowe, 52, a performer and songwriter who started Renaissance Enterprises in 1988 in Portage, Michigan. Through the nonprofit organization, nearly 30 musicians, theatrical performers, storytellers, painters, and clowns bring the arts to shut-ins by presenting more than 200 shows yearly at nursing homes and other institutions in Michigan and surrounding states. Contributions from churches and other organizations, and sales from Rowe's CDs, help defray their costs.

Through the years, Rowe has witnessed hundreds of smiles light up the faces of withdrawn seniors and disabled residents as he croons such coax-a-grin classics as "Let Me Call You Sweetheart" and "Goodnight Irene." He's seen elderly patients with Alzheimer's disease, who couldn't recall their own names, sing the entire lyrics to "You Are My Sunshine" without skipping a beat.

"We've had residents with dementia who were so agitated and irritable we didn't know if they could stay for the performance," says Ronda Bolin, activity therapy leader for Lakeland Continuing Care in St. Joseph, Michigan. "Then Bob starts interacting with them, and soon they are laughing and smiling. He takes them to a happier place."

Rowe says such testimonies speak to the nurturing power of music and the arts. "We explain to contributors all the time that this is not pure entertainment," says Rowe. "This is really therapy because it has a definite cognitive effect on the people we serve and on their quality of life and spiritual, mental, and emotional well-being."

Rowe and his fellow entertainers sing nostalgic favorites from the 1930s and '40s such as "As Time Goes By," gospel standards like "The Old Rugged Cross" and "How Great Thou Art," and seasonal songs for Christmas, Easter, and other holidays. He insists that performers who volunteer through Renaissance Enterprises have "the right heart."

"Bob knows many residents by name, and he sings to them and makes them feel very special," says Kathy Libbrecht, activity director at Park Place Assisted Living Center in Kalamazoo.

In September 2006, the St. Bernadette Institute of Sacred Art in New Mexico named Rowe a 2006 Mother Teresa Laureate, citing his work and adding him to a prestigious list of previous laureates that includes former president Jimmy Carter, Archbishop Desmond Tutu, and poet Maya Angelou.

The honor is particularly meaningful to Rowe since he actually corresponded with Mother Teresa beginning in the late 1980s, receiving 15 letters from the beloved humanitarian. He cherishes a 1992 letter in which Mother Teresa wrote, "Your work of love in nursing homes, hospitals, for the aged, the neglected and the forgotten is truly the work of peace."

Rowe says he always has felt "blessed" to perform for the elderly and disabled. As the oldest of six children growing up in Battle Creek, Michigan, he was especially close to both of his grandmothers, one of whom helped care for Rowe's family for many years after his father suffered a heart attack. A great-aunt with two developmentally disabled sons further instilled his compassion for others.

"I saw my great-aunt in her 80s pushing two grown men to the toilet in their wheelchairs and shaving and feeding them without complaining," Rowe recalls.

When he was a teenager at Battle Creek's St. Philip Catholic Central High School, he accompanied the nuns to play guitar for shut-ins. Later, when traveling the country on the club circuit as a folk singer, he gave volunteer performances at local nursing homes.

"In 1980, I got a contract with a Catholic music publisher to publish my inspirational music in hymnals," Rowe says. "This is when I realized I wanted to do something more meaningful with my life."

After a show, nursing home residents with canes, walkers, and in wheelchairs file past Rowe to shake his hand, hug him, and ask for an encore visit. They look like parishioners thanking their pastor after a particularly touching sermon, which is not surprising.

When Rowe was younger, he wanted to be a priest. Now he has his own musical ministry, one that gives him the chance to witness miracles almost every time he plays.

—Karen Karvonen

By using our natural gifts and talents to connect with others, we become a catalyst of hope and change for all generations.

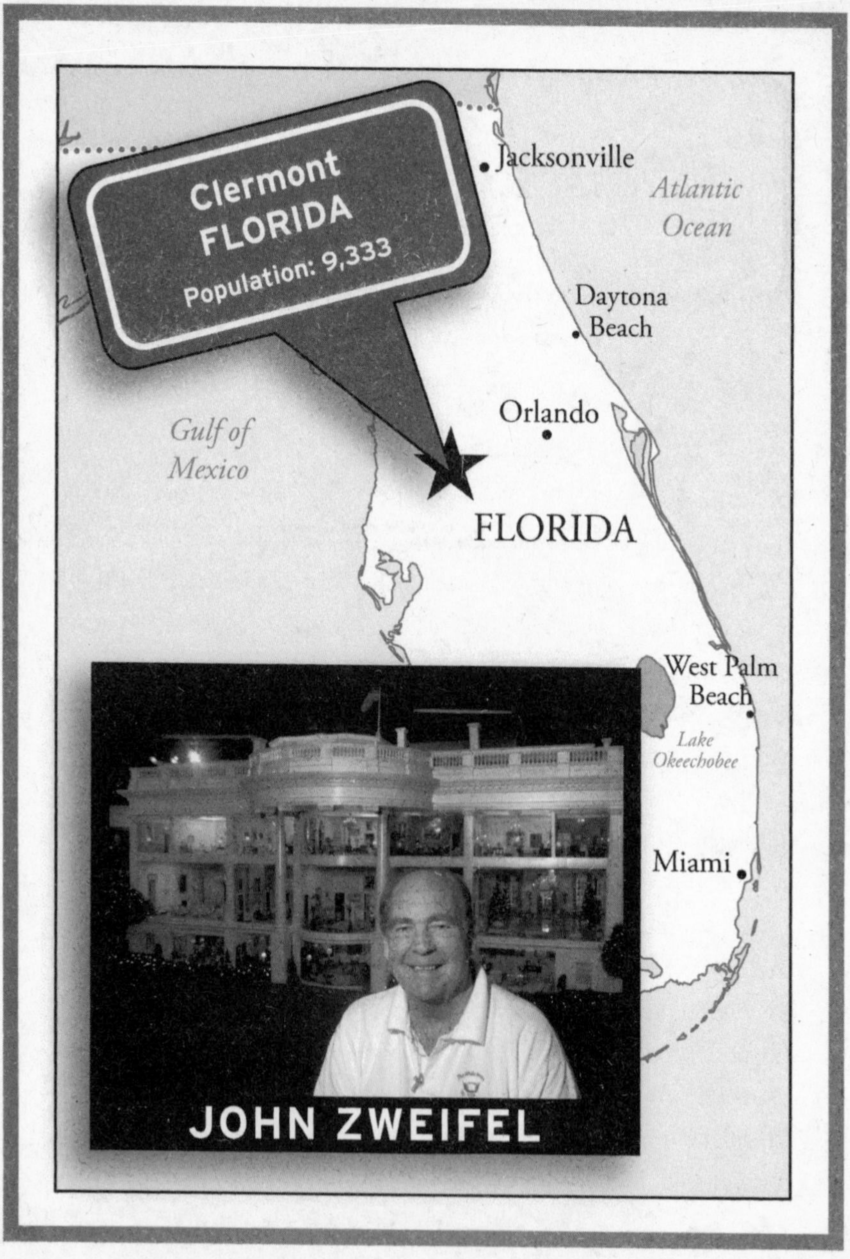

Clermont
FLORIDA
Population: 9,333

Jacksonville

Atlantic Ocean

Daytona Beach

Orlando

Gulf of Mexico

FLORIDA

West Palm Beach

Lake Okeechobee

Miami

JOHN ZWEIFEL

A Gift to the Nation

At age 20, John Zweifel visited the White House and toured the five rooms that are open to the public, but longed to see the rest of the official residence of our nation's presidents.

The experience laid the cornerstone for his lifelong labor of love—a 60-by-20-foot replica of the White House that has traveled to all 50 states and been visited by millions of people who may never step inside the mansion at 1600 Pennsylvania Avenue in Washington, D.C.

"I want to give people the feeling that the president called up and said, 'Come on over,'" says John, 70. "The White House transcends politics. It's the people's house."

John and his wife, Jan, began building the 1-inch-to-1-foot scale model in 1962. In the years since, they have spent more than $1 million creating tiny moldings, mantels, portraits, and pieces of furniture for their White House in miniature. When the 10-ton mansion is not on tour, its permanent home is at the couple's Presidents Hall of Fame in Clermont, Florida, near their home in Orlando.

"It's just gorgeous," said Helen Lombardo, of Overland Park, Kansas, viewing the replica White House during a 2006 exhibition at the Truman Presidential Museum and Library in Independence, Missouri.

Lights glow, telephones ring, televisions play, clocks tick, and the water fountain in the Jacqueline Kennedy Garden flows. The State Dining Room is set for 80 guests with gold-painted pewter chairs that weigh 3 ounces each. Glassblowers spent three months making wine, water, and champagne glasses for the tables. An army of craftspeople has helped with the project.

The chandeliers in the East Room are hand-blown glass with 55 lightbulbs, each the size of a grain of rice with hairlike electrical wires. It takes five hours to change the chandeliers' delicate bulbs.

The Zweifels' six children joined the family mission as they grew old enough to help. Oldest son Jack spent hundreds of hours carving the most intricate piece, a replica of the rosewood table in the Lincoln Bedroom. The 2½-inch-tall marble-topped table has storks carved in the legs and grape clusters fringing the tabletop. John carved the replica of the famous 6-by-9-foot Lincoln bed.

Work on the miniature White House is never finished. Each time the Oval Office is redecorated by its new occupant, identical changes are made to the Zweifels' small-scale model.

"My favorite Oval Office was [Richard] Nixon's," Jan says, "because it was all in royal blue and gold, probably the most regal of them all."

One of her favorite comments about their creation came from future president Bill Clinton, who opened the exhibit in 1979 in Little Rock when he was governor of Arkansas. "He pointed to the replica and said, 'Someday, I'm going to live in that house.'"

The Zweifels did "live" at the White House for two weeks in 1975, taking photographs and measurements. Before then, they worked from photographs and details memorized during public tours, sometimes four a day. "Every president since [Gerald] Ford has patted me on the back and said, 'Keep going,'" John says.

Building the White House replica seemed like a natural project to John, who by age 6 was carving tiny ponies and trapeze artists for circus scenes to entertain his invalid grandmother. By 15, John was creating window displays for Chicago department stores and has worked ever since in the display and entertainment business. His passion, though, has been building the White House in miniature and taking it to the people.

"It's a very, very accurate re-creation of the White House," says Rex Scouten of Fairfax, Virginia, who retired as White House curator in 1998. "It's a magnificent gift to the nation."

—Marti Attoun

A boundless love of country is an honorable attribute and can be lived out in tasks that we perform with enthusiasm and excellence.

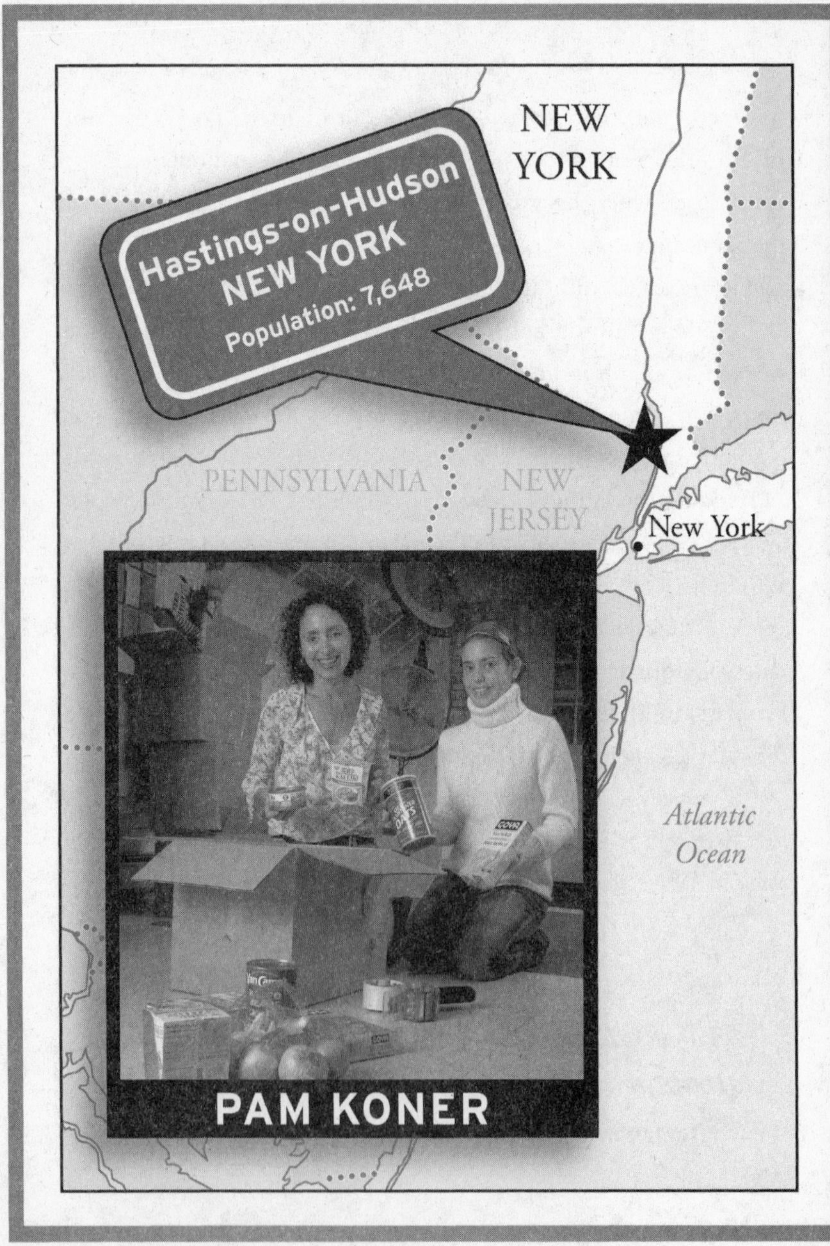

NEW YORK

Hastings-on-Hudson
NEW YORK
Population: 7,648

PENNSYLVANIA

NEW JERSEY

New York

Atlantic Ocean

PAM KONER

Fostering Family Ties

Pam Koner was reading the Sunday newspaper on her deck in 2002 when she spotted a photograph of a girl sitting on a filthy mattress, eating her one meal of the day—pasta with chicken neck bones. A story accompanying the photograph described one of the nation's poorest places: Pembroke, a township in Kankakee County, Illinois.

What moved Koner most was learning that at the end of each month, the shelves of the only local food pantry, in Hopkins Park, Illinois, were empty and some families barely had enough to eat. "When I walked off my deck that day, I said, 'I've got to do something,'" recalls Koner, 55, owner and director of several creative arts–based childcare programs in Hastings-on-Hudson, New York.

It didn't take long for Koner to figure out a way to help. She called the pastor of the Church of the Cross, which runs the food pantry in Hopkins Park, and pitched her idea. "I said, 'What if I have families in my community adopt families in yours and send them one week of food when the food pantry's empty?'

"I'm the mother of adopted children," she added, referring to her girls, Olivia, 19, and Chloe, 16. "To me, the word adoption means 'to make families.'"

Within a few weeks, Koner had the names of 17 families in Pembroke Township willing to be adopted, and she recruited neighbors and friends in her hometown to serve as donors. Within a month, she had linked 34 families, and the Family-to-Family program was born.

Today, through word of mouth and media coverage, the program has grown to more than 475 donor families who send monthly food parcels to 475 recipient families in 15 communities in Arkansas, Illinois, Kentucky, Louisiana, Maine, Mississippi, New Mexico, New York, South Dakota, and West Virginia. "Our mission is to have 20 communities by next year," Koner says.

Each month, donor families log on to her Web site—www.family-to-family.com—to access their monthly shopping lists, which includes items such as soup, pasta, tuna fish, and other pre-packaged food. In addition to food, the program encourages donors to send needed items such as over-the-counter medications, sheets, towels, clothing, and back-to-school supplies. The monthly cost per donor family averages $35 to $40. Federal Express ships more than 500 Family-to-Family food packages free of charge each month.

Lori Ratner of Stamford, Connecticut, has been involved with Family-to-Family since 2004. "Without doing much, you're doing so much," Ratner says. "It's had a big impact, not only on myself, but also on my husband and my four kids. It shows them you can give in more ways than just giving money, and it shows them that little things do make a difference."

Koner acknowledges it takes time to shop for another family and package the food every month, but she does it because it's more meaningful than sending money, and it provides an important message about caring and compassion to her children.

"It's easy to write a check, but it's not always easy to do the right thing when you're busy," she says. "I came up with something that is hands-on. We're teaching our children that giving often has some sense of personal sacrifice. This creates a sense of living empathy."

So does the letter writing in which Koner strongly encourages both donor and recipient families to participate. "There is no middle-person charity. I pack my box, I put my letter in, and the person who opens it up and puts on my daughter's jacket is my family. My family and I will always stay connected."

Lisa Dyson, a pastor at Church of the Cross, says the relationship between donor and recipient families is just as important as what's packed in the boxes. "It sends a message that somebody cares, and that somebody thought of them time after time. Some of them have had the same families for almost four years. The Family-to-Family program expands their horizons."

—Debbe Geiger

"If you can't feed a hundred people, then feed just one." —Mother Teresa

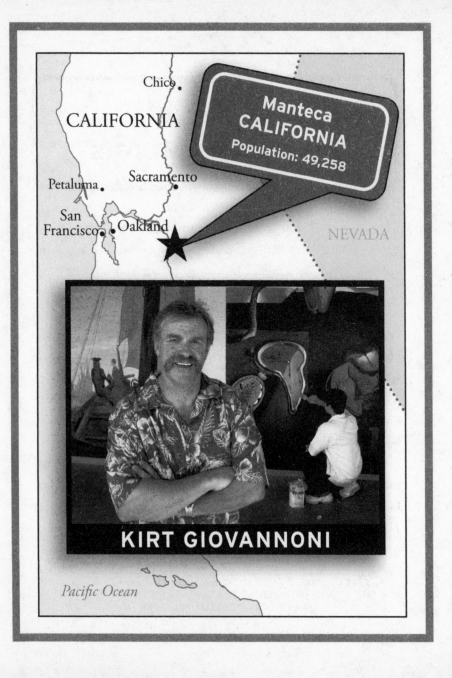

Chico

CALIFORNIA

Manteca
CALIFORNIA
Population: 49,258

Petaluma

Sacramento

San Francisco

Oakland

NEVADA

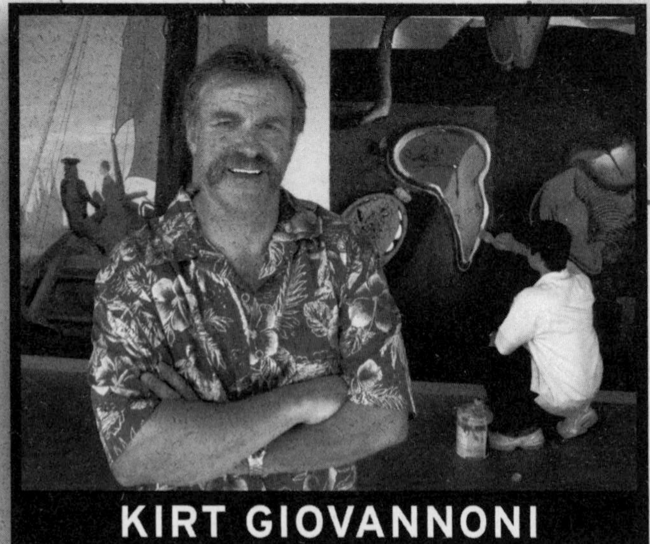

KIRT GIOVANNONI

Pacific Ocean

Master of Manteca's Murals

In 1996, art teacher Kirt Giovannoni was fed up with the destructive and demoralizing graffiti that frequently appeared on the campus of Manteca (California) High School. So he devised a plan—dubbed The Mural Project—to discourage and replace the unsightly spray-painted mess with student-painted re-creations of famous works of art.

Eleven years later, The Mural Project has produced 144 murals—some as large as 8-feet-by-7-feet—at the Manteca high school, where Edouard Manet's 1866 masterpiece, *The Fife Player,* shares wall space with Andy Warhol's 1962 cutting-edge *Soup Cans.* School groups and art lovers from throughout the state tour the eclectic collection. Best of all, graffiti has become a rarity and school pride is on the rise.

"We're respected for the work we do on the murals," says Mark Ryser, who graduated from Manteca High in 2006 after taking Giovannoni's advanced art class as a senior. "Usually, it's an accident if a pencil mark shows up or a mural gets scuffed."

Each year, Giovannoni, known to students as "Mr. G," breaks his class into teams of three and assigns each a particular wall space in the school for their mural. That's when the research begins.

"The kids interview the teachers whose rooms are near the proposed murals to get an idea of any special elements, like science or music, that should go into the selected picture," says Giovannoni, 51, who's been a teacher for 28 years. "Then they go through art history books, the senior students present a few of their ideas, and I'll usually narrow the choices down to a final dozen that's reviewed by school administrators."

Next, Giovannoni and his teacher assistants clean the walls of the work area and create chalked grid lines to guide students as they transfer the work of art from its original scale to a mural.

"Working on the murals is just like having a job," says Daniel Sanchez, a recently graduated student who is now majoring in art at a local community college. "We have a lot of room to express ourselves, and Mr. G really shows us how to push ourselves."

Teams have only seven to eight weeks, working 55 minutes each school day, to finish their projects. If they procrastinate, pace themselves poorly, or don't learn to work together, the space is painted over—something that's happened only twice, Sanchez says.

Taking original art and reproducing it on a large wall can be just as daunting as figuring out how to work with project teammates, says senior Trevor Neuner. While his love of art leans toward commercial art and comic books, Neuner took in stride his team's assignment of re-creating an oil painting of frothy ocean waves and boats by German artist Eugene Garin. And even though a crack in the school wall and a metal electrical box in his mural's grid gave Neuner pause, he managed to work them into the mural's background and complete the painting in 2006.

It's this flexibility, along with the chance to discover new elements—both in the art they're reproducing and in themselves—that's at the heart of Giovannoni's program.

"The Mural Project gives the kids a test run of the real world, as once they're on the teams, they can't move out," Giovannoni says. "If they have problems with each other in terms of the mural, they have a chance to work on communication and team-building, two skills I hope they take with them when they leave the class."

Gayl Wilson, treasurer and a founder of the Manteca Mural Society, a nonprofit organization that commissions large paintings on the city's downtown buildings, isn't surprised that The Mural Project's educational value reaches beyond the art students themselves.

"With all the TV and mass media teenagers watch, I don't imagine they see much art," Wilson says. "But the students who are just walking down the hall to math or biology get exposed to a huge amount and variety of art they might never see in their lifetime otherwise. Plus, people who attend adult education classes at the high school see the murals. Now that's a cool thing to find here in Manteca!"

—DEBI DRAKE

With a little imagination, you can transform irritating messes into thoughtfully crafted treasures.

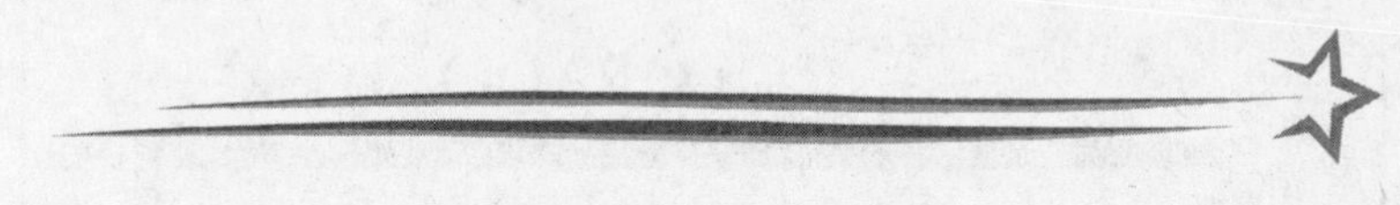

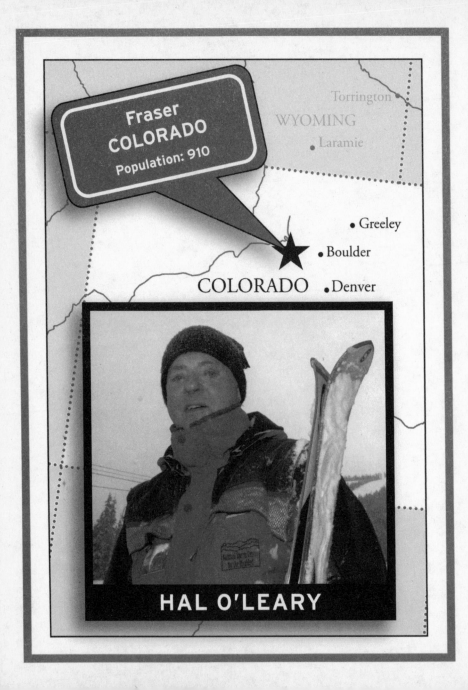

Fraser
COLORADO
Population: 910

Torrington
WYOMING
Laramie
Greeley
Boulder
COLORADO
Denver

HAL O'LEARY

Enabling Disabled Skiers

Nothing thrills ski instructor Hal O'Leary more than seeing a dozen empty wheelchairs parked at the base of the ski slopes in Winter Park, Colorado. "I see people who are double amputees or paraplegics get out of their car, pull out their wheelchair and mono-ski [a molded seat mounted on a single ski with hand-held outrigger ski tips], and proceed to the lift all by themselves," O'Leary says.

Minutes later, they are whizzing down the runs using adaptive ski equipment that O'Leary helped develop.

Since founding the National Sports Center for the Disabled (NSCD) in 1970, O'Leary has made it possible for thousands of kids and adults with close to 100 different disabilities—including birth defects, multiple sclerosis, autism, developmental disabilities, and blindness—to enjoy the snow-covered slopes. Today, the NSCD gives more than 7,000 ski lessons a year, and other programs worldwide refer people to the center.

O'Leary, 68, vividly recalls teaching his very first adaptive ski lesson—to 23 young amputees from Children's Hospital in Denver—in 1970. A ski instructor in Winter Park, he had volunteered to help the hospital's amputee program though, at the time, no specific method existed for teaching amputees to ski.

"It was a cold, miserable January day, and the kids were slipping and sliding," recalls O'Leary, who lives in nearby Fraser, Colorado. "After lunch I put them on the chair lift, and it was a melee at the top. But as we started working on the practice hill, they began moving on their own and squealing with excitement."

O'Leary was hooked, and his new dream was to inspire and enable disabled individuals to enjoy the sport he loves. He began to devise his own methods and equipment, developing the three-track system for amputees who use one ski and two outriggers, forearm crutches with ski tips mounted to the bases.

When teaching a child with spina bifida who had great difficulty standing, O'Leary devised a contraption called the ski bra. "Larry's skis kept parting and going out, and he would fall forward," O'Leary says. "So I put a hole in the tips of the skis and threaded a bungee cord through them to stabilize them. He was able to ski and turn without falling, and now I see it used wherever I go."

A former coach of the U.S. Disabled Olympic Ski Team, O'Leary pioneered competitive racing for the disabled. One of his star pupils, David Jamison of Tabernash, Colorado, the 1982 U.S. World Champion in the slalom category, went on to race competitively for 22 years.

A three-tracker with polio in his left leg, Jamison started skiing with O'Leary in 1971. "Without him, I wouldn't have gotten to the level of skiing I did, and the racing program wouldn't have become world class," Jamison says.

Despite O'Leary's success with his students, his first 10 years were a struggle. "People who felt that skiing was for the 'able-bodied' criticized me," O'Leary says. That mind-set changed, however, after his adaptive ski program was featured on the *Today* and *Good Morning America* television shows and began to gain national recognition.

In the past 36 years, O'Leary has not only enabled thousands to ski, he's touched lives and often changed their course. Susan Hildebrecht of Boulder, Colorado, who has cerebral palsy and skis with a ski bra and two outriggers, took lessons from O'Leary as a 16-year-old in 1977. "Hal is a phenomenal teacher with a sixth sense. He can tell you, 'Let's do this,' and nine out of 10 times, it works," she says.

With O'Leary's support and encouragement, Hildebrecht passed the Professional Ski Instructors of America course and taught in Winter Park's adaptive ski program for 15 years.

"Hal's teaching goes beyond skiing," says Jamison, who now works in real estate. "He's been a coach, a mentor, and a friend. He has taught me that I could achieve anything I put my mind to, and that has helped me be successful in my business."

As adaptive skiing gained momentum, O'Leary has traveled worldwide to help establish programs for the disabled and is a recipient of the prestigious Professional Ski Instructor of America Lifetime Achievement Award. But he still gets the most satisfaction out of seeing a kid who walks with crutches glide down a slope with a big grin on his face.

"I've gotten a lot more out of this than I have put in over these 36 years," O'Leary says. "And I'll keep on teaching as long as I am upright."

—Karen Karvonen

If you enjoy an activity, find a way to share it with people who are excluded from that experience for one reason or another, and you will be rewarded a hundred times over.

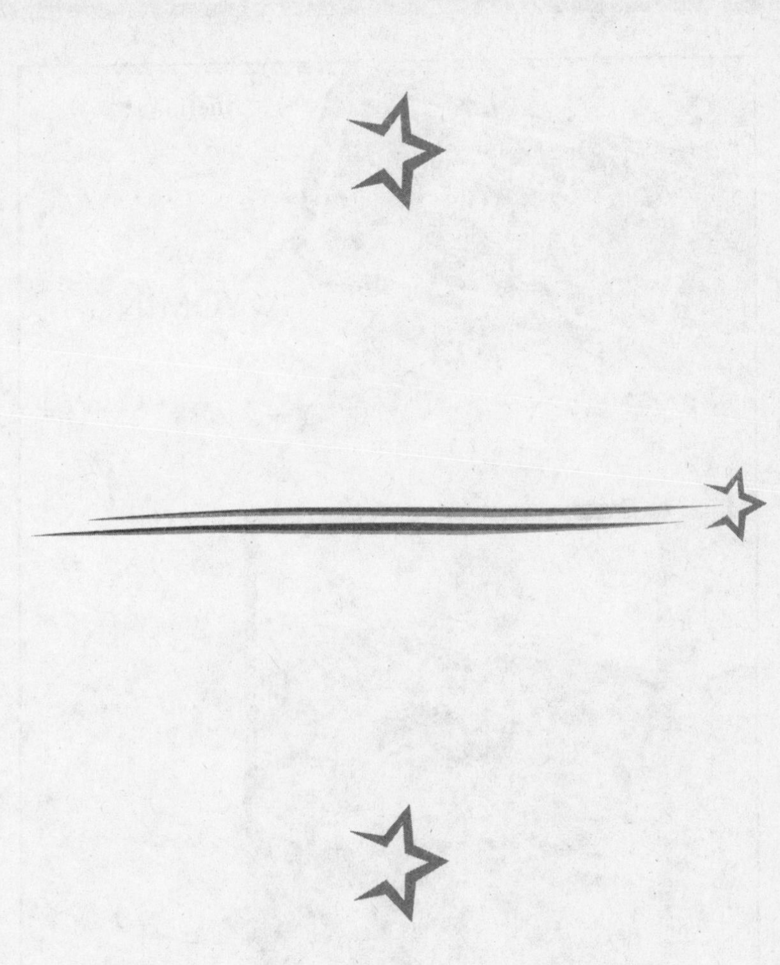

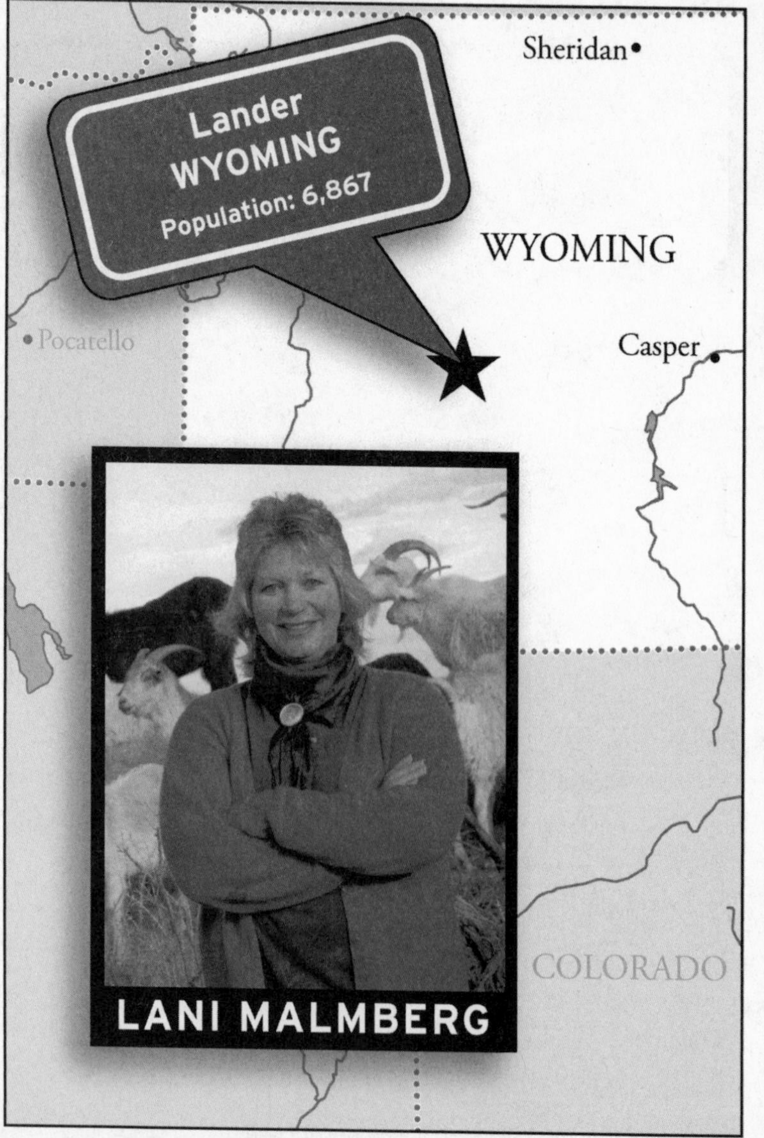
Lander
WYOMING
Population: 6,867
Sheridan
WYOMING
Pocatello
Casper
COLORADO
LANI MALMBERG

Devouring the West's Weeds

Lani Malmberg wanders the meadows, hillsides, and waterways of the West, hooked staff in hand, pitting 1,900 cashmere goats against pockets of unwanted weeds that infest the landscape.

A full-time traveling goat herder with a master's degree in weed science, she works out of a travel camper where she also sleeps. But Malmberg, 49, lives largely outdoors under open skies, herding goats from one patch of wild weeds to another with the help of five canine companions.

"Bring 'em back, Bru," Malmberg calls to her lead herding dog. The Border collie jumps out of the bushes, looks around, then dashes to nip two straggling goats back toward the herd. Task completed, Malmberg coos, "That'll do Bru," then finally barks, "Down!" to get the hard-working dog to stop and rest.

Malmberg believes weeds are a symptom of an ecological imbalance, and her goats help restore the land to a natural state. "My higher education mostly qualifies me to hawk chemicals," Malmberg says, "but I want people to know they have better options."

Her business is full service. Before setting her goats to graze, Malmberg seeds the land with native grasses. Employees help set portable electric fences, then Malmberg unloads her animals from four large four-deck semi-trailers. While the goats munch the weeds and fertilize the seeds, they mulch and aerate the soil with their tiny hooves. Malmberg says weeds are the goats' gourmet food of choice, and they seem to know which plants belong there and which ones don't.

"The weeds are smarter than the native plants, the goats are smarter than the weeds, and the only things smarter than the goats are the Border collies," she says.

Malmberg uses her brother's ranch address in Lander, Wyoming, as her own, but she's rarely there. Instead, she travels like a gypsy from one job to another in any of 10 Western states from Kansas to California.

Her company, Ewe4ic Ecological Services, has a list of repeat clients, from municipal governments to private landowners to homeowners associations. She tends the goats year-round, staying at each location from a few weeks to several months. A hundred goats can graze an acre a day, and Malmberg's fees start at about a dollar a day for each goat.

The cost of each job depends on the nature and location of the weeds, a subject Malmberg knows well. In fact, she says she's kind of a weed herself, living off other people's land and spreading her eco-friendly philosophy as she goes. Unlike a weed though, Malmberg and her goats leave the land better than they found it.

Originally from Nebraska and then Wyoming, Malmberg left the family ranch in the late 1980s when poor economic conditions crippled many small ranches. She returned to school at age 33, earning degrees in environmental restoration, biology/botany, and eventually weed science at Colorado State University. In 1998, she launched her unique business, borrowing money against her pickup truck and her sons' college savings to buy her first 100 goats.

Word of Malmberg's weed-eating goats spread like, well, weeds. It turns out her service is sorely needed to keep weeds from taking over large tracts of land, especially in places with rugged rock crevices and steep, craggy hillsides, and in areas close to water where city laws and public concern prevent the use of chemical weed control.

Robert A. Lee, a zoologist and director of environmental management for the city of Cheyenne, Wyoming, and a regular client, credits Malmberg's goats with reducing Cheyenne's overall weed infestation by more than 50 percent—without using a drop of herbicide. He has received hundreds of calls from citizens thanking him for using four-legged weed control over chemical options. "I'm amazed at how many people actually care that we aren't taking a chance on polluting the water," he says.

The animals are also popular in Cheyenne with families and children, who often visit the goat camp and bring Malmberg donuts and covered dishes.

"The goats are great," Lee says. "Our mayor once called them our part-time summer employees. But Lani Malmberg's weed science expertise is what sold us. She didn't just fall off the turnip truck."

When she's not guiding her animals to new grazing plots and shepherding her herd, Malmberg's chores include watering the goats, tending an occasional wound, or bottle-feeding an orphaned kid. In between jobs, she teaches weed management workshops and helps people start their own eco-friendly goat businesses. Fifteen families have launched similar ventures under her tutelage, though Malmberg's service remains unique.

"I'm the only one who travels, the only one with a master's degree in weed science, and the only one who makes a full-time living at it," she says. "I make my sole income from this, so it's very important to me to do the job right every time."

—Kathy Summers

If you follow your natural instincts, you're more likely to find balance and peace and purpose in your life.

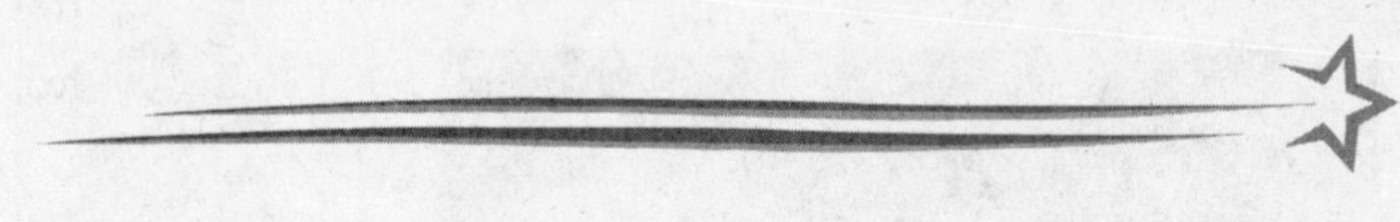

JOHN STEEVES

Taking the Bible Behind Bars

The men who study the Bible with John Steeves aren't your average churchgoers. Dressed in orange prison garb, many await sentencing for burglary, trafficking in narcotics, rape, and murder.

But that doesn't faze Steeves, 83, a World War II veteran and volunteer minister from Neenah, Wisconsin. For nearly 45 years, he has spent three days a week spreading the Gospel and straight talk to inmates at the Winnebago County Jail in nearby Oshkosh.

"I was a high school teacher and had a family of eight to support, so my time was limited. But I thought it was something I could do to serve God," says Steeves, who responded to a fellow parishioner's request at his local church to lead Bible studies in the county jail. "That was in '62, and I'm thankful for the opportunity and heart for this work that God has given me."

Steeves is undaunted by the fact that nearly 75 percent of the men he counsels return to lives of crime after their release. He believes the Lord gives second chances—and third, fourth, and fifth chances as well. He teaches that redemption and salvation are possible if people truly want to change, and accepts the reality that some, sadly, do not.

"Some of them read and understand the Bible very well," Steeves says. "The trouble is they are good at talking about the Bible, but they aren't living it. I always stress that they need to walk the talk."

A soft-spoken, grandfatherly man, Steeves may seem an unlikely candidate for a jail ministry. But as a young U.S. Army recruit, he long ago witnessed mankind at its worst. The young soldier landed on the beach of Normandy, France, in 1944, and was wounded in the D-Day invasion. After recuperating for a month and a half, he fought in three more battles.

"I've seen what men like Hitler, who didn't follow the truth of the Bible, could do," Steeves says.

Steeves also knows firsthand what a difference that a helping hand can make. When he was 5, his parents broke up, and he was given up for adoption. "The family that took me in was a blessing," Steeves says, "I could tell God was watching out for me from the beginning."

Through the years, Steeves has steered many men toward a spiritual path.

Fred Sowatzka, 60, began attending Steeves' Bible studies in 1971 when he was jailed and battling addictions to drugs and alcohol. "He really changed my life," says Sowatzka, who even joined his mentor's church when he was released. Sowatzka has since started a jail ministry of his own and, for the last 12 years, has provided religious guidance at the nearby Outagamie County Justice Center in Appleton, Wisconsin, where he is full-time chaplain director for the 550 inmates there.

Ed Demler, a chaplain with the Winnebago County Sheriff's Department, estimates that Steeves' jail ministry has touched at least 66,000 people. "It's so inspiring for me to see a man who is so committed," Demler says. "John never gives up on people."

Steeves finds great satisfaction in bumping into the inmates he's helped in the community. "Wherever I go, I run into people who say 'Hey sir, remember me from jail?'" Steeves says. "It's hard for me to remember everyone, but I know that the Lord is working in their lives, and I know that my life has been so worthwhile because of the time I've spent in His ministry."

—KAREN KARVONEN

Make time each week to volunteer and serve others. It's great exercise for the heart.

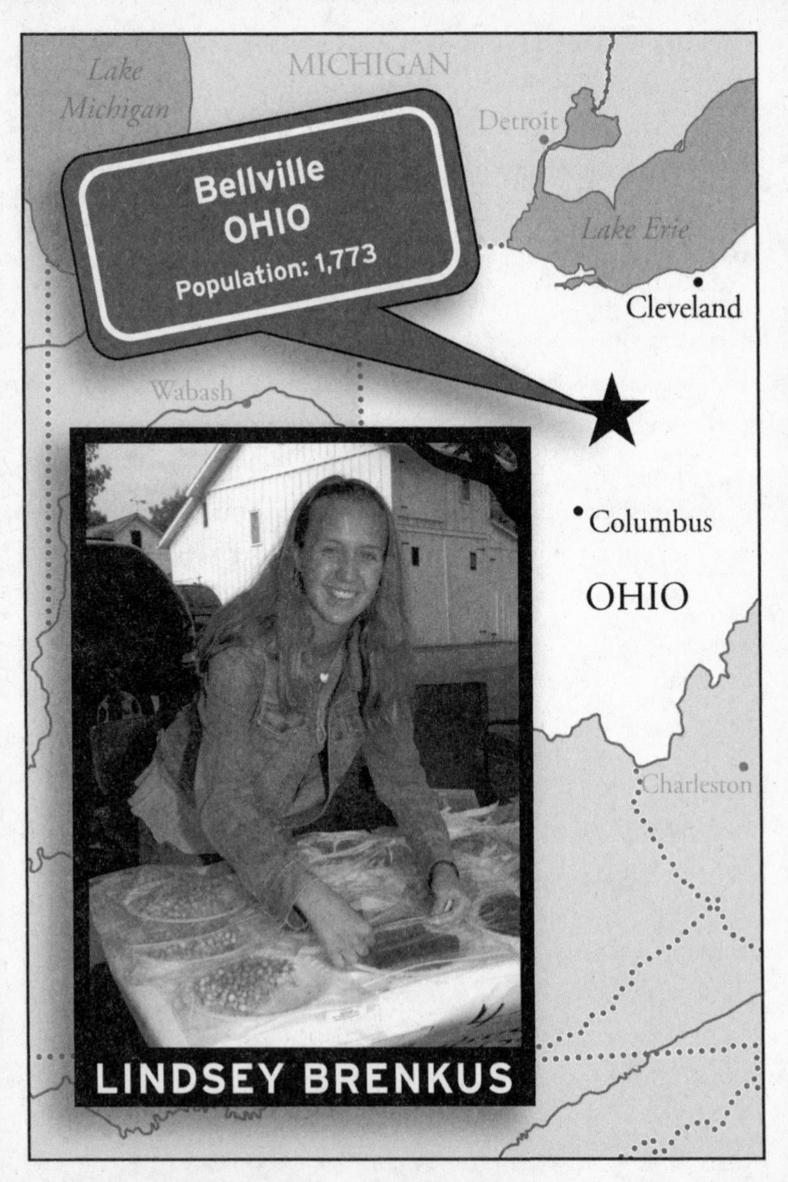
Lake Michigan
MICHIGAN
Detroit
Bellville
OHIO
Population: 1,773
Lake Erie
Cleveland
Wabash
Columbus
OHIO
Charleston
LINDSEY BRENKUS

Hosting the Farmers Market

Lindsey Brenkus surveys a tub of homegrown lettuce, loaves of just-baked wheat bread, and tables heaped with pickles, parsley, onions, and oatmeal cookies. She can't stop smiling. It's another blue-ribbon day at the farmers market in Bellville, Ohio.

Just 14, Lindsey is an old hand at managing the Bellville Farmers Market, which she founded in 2003.

"My grandma took me to a farmers market in Mount Vernon [Ohio] when I was 9, and it was great and I loved it," Lindsey recalls. "I bought a dill plant and some tomatoes. I was like, 'Grandma, why doesn't Bellville have a farmers market?'"

Her grandmother, Pam Wolfe, remembers the conversation. "I said, 'because someone has to start it.'"

The seed was planted and Lindsey, then a fourth-grader at Bellville Elementary School, didn't stop until she had established a full-grown farmers market in her hometown.

Her mother, Teri Brenkus, laughs when people praise her for being a supportive parent. "I tried to ignore Lindsey," Teri admits, "but she bugged me to death. She kept saying, 'Who do I call next?'"

To learn about running a farmers market, Lindsey called directors of nearby markets, the Richland County Health Department, and the Ohio Department of Agriculture. Then she met with the Bellville City Council.

Councilman William Sheriff says the young girl's enthusiasm won them over. "She was all keyed up. She gave us a presentation and everyone thought it was just great," Sheriff says while selling hazelnuts and flavored popcorn at the farmers market. "The town's glad to have her out here. We get a lot of compliments on her."

On Saturday mornings from June through October, as many as 30 farmers and gardeners set up tables under the towering maples on the Bellville town square. Lindsey marks off 10-by-10-foot spaces, which cost $5 apiece for the season. Fees are paid to the city. Vendors agree to guidelines that specify the hours of operation, what can be sold, and cleanup duties. Lindsey enforces the rules.

"One guy tried to sell birdhouses," says Lindsey, who prohibits the selling of crafts. "I want to keep the farmers market natural."

With Lindsey at the helm, the Bellville Farmers Market has blossomed into more than a place to buy just-picked peppers and pumpkins.

"It's turned into a social event for this town," says Dave Duncan of nearby Crestline, who peddles honey and beeswax-based soaps and lotions. "I'm tickled about this market and enjoy calling a 14-year-old my boss."

For vendors, the extra income they've earned is much appreciated. "On a busy day, you can take in two or three hundred dollars," says Mick Conrad from nearby Mansfield, who sells pickles, jellies, and relishes.

To advertise the Bellville Farmers Market, Lindsey displays fliers at downtown businesses and posts hand-painted road signs with help from her father, Mike Brenkus. For a while, she enlisted help from her brothers, Mikey, 12, and Stuart, 10.

"I paid my little brothers a dollar an hour to dance out on the sidewalk with the farmers market sign. Then they wanted $2 an hour," says Lindsey, who outsourced their job to some neighbor kids.

Lindsey sells her own homegrown tomatoes and fresh herbs, along with zucchini bread and chocolate chip cookies, which always sell out at $2.50 a half-dozen. Last summer, she helped her brother Stuart bake his own chocolate chip cookies.

"I didn't give him a nudge. I gave him a push," says Lindsey, who ended up doing the bulk of the baking.

In the spirit of free enterprise, Stuart undersold his sister, selling his cookies at $2 for five. Lindsey didn't complain much. She knows it's in the best interest of the market, which has been a blooming success from the start—thanks to her pure-hearted spirit and dogged determination.

"Lindsey doesn't have any greed in mind," beekeeper Duncan says. "She just wanted to do something nice for her community."

—Marti Attoun

There's no stopping a kid with a great idea and a bushel of love for her community.

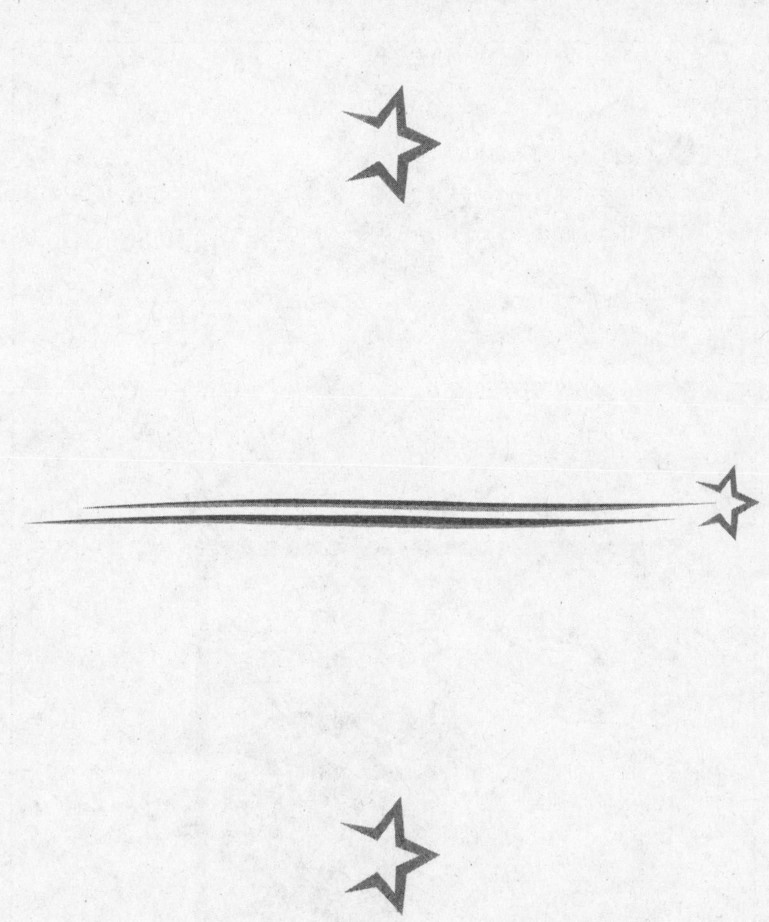

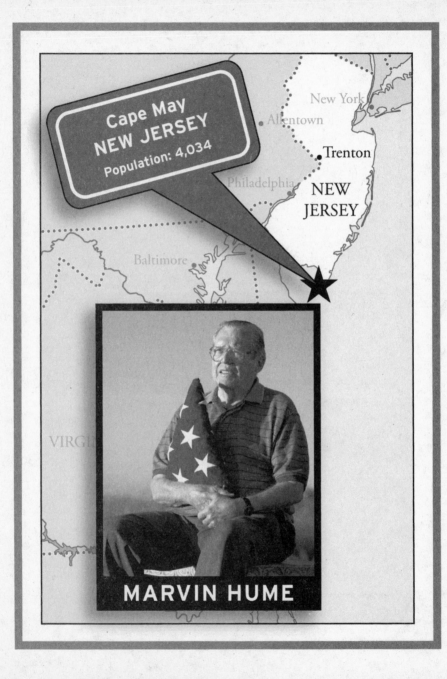

Cape May
NEW JERSEY
Population: 4,034

New York
Allentown
Trenton
Philadelphia
NEW JERSEY
Baltimore

MARVIN HUME

A Sunset Beach Salute

Marvin Hume was a 20-year-old college student in December 1941 when he learned that two buddies had been killed during the Japanese bombing of Pearl Harbor. Joseph Hittorff and Walter Simon were Hume's childhood friends from Collingswood, New Jersey. They died on a Sunday morning two and a half weeks before Christmas amid a cascade of bombs that killed more than 2,300 Americans.

Hume was fuming with rage; his desire to enter the military "was absolute." He enlisted and served in the U.S. Navy for three years and, during his missions, saw unforgettable images of death and destruction on islands in the South Pacific.

Hume, 86, doesn't talk much nowadays about those World War II images, but they are at the heart of a memorial ceremony he has conducted since 1973 just outside the beachside resort town of Cape May, New Jersey. From May to October, Hume conducts a daily flag ceremony on Sunset Beach to honor the sacrifices of the nation's war veterans.

Fifteen minutes before sunset, Hume stands at the base of a flagpole on Sunset Beach, alongside a family that wishes to honor a deceased loved one who served in the military. As the sun prepares to touch the horizon over Delaware Bay, Hume plays "God Bless America" and "The Star-Spangled Banner" over a loudspeaker system, then helps members of the family lower the American flag while "Taps" is played.

Hundreds of beachgoers stand at attention during the songs, many of them with tears in their eyes.

"It's so honorable and patriotic," says Gary LeFevre of Hanover, Pennsylvania, attending a ceremony in 2005 honoring his late grandfather, Clyde LeFevre, who served in the U.S. Air Force during World War II. "I wanted to instill this in my children's life," says LeFevre, attending the ceremony with his wife, Amy, and their three children, along with three other family members.

Hume never could have scripted the story of how he came to conduct the ceremony. After World War II, he worked for an aircraft company in St. Louis. But his passion was collecting minerals and, in 1957, Hume gave up his engineering career to start a rock and shell shop in Atlantic City, New Jersey. Over the next 15 years, he developed a successful store and wholesale business. One day, while Hume was making a delivery to Sunset Beach, Preston Shadbolt, the owner of a shell and mineral shop, asked if Hume wanted to buy the place. Hume agreed to a price, and they sealed the deal with a handshake.

Shadbolt, who had served in the Army during World War II, asked Hume for one favor: continue his ritual of playing Kate Smith's version of "God Bless America"—a song he loved—each night at sunset while lowering Old Glory. Hume honored Shadbolt's request, but took it a step further: he placed an ad in a local newspaper asking for casket flags to fly on Sunset Beach. "I've never had to advertise since," he says.

More than three decades later, Hume and his family run three gift shops and lease a restaurant at the end of Sunset Boulevard. Many flag-ceremony participants ask for the chance to lower their loved one's casket flag, while others, who have not lost a loved one in battle, volunteer to lower one of the donated casket flags that Hume keeps in storage.

Americans, ranging from military generals to church camp participants, have lowered flags at Sunset Beach, and they've honored veterans from military engagements ranging from World War I to the war in Iraq. Hume recalls one recent flag volunteer, a nearly blind boy with multiple sclerosis. When the flag fell into his hands, the boy started crying.

"He said, 'This is the proudest moment of my life,'" Hume recalls. "The American flag in his hands had honored someone who had served his country."

The flag ceremony has become so popular that the summertime months are often booked a year in advance by families wishing to honor their loved ones.

Hume shrugs off any notion that he's a hero. He'd rather praise his childhood buddies, Hittorff and Simon, who made the ultimate sacrifice. "I don't do it for accolades," Hume says. "I do it because of how I feel inside."

—Warren Hynes

A golden moment of quiet respect not only honors those who have served their country but inspires courage and patriotism in countless others.

Contributors

The following writers contributed to this book:

Chuck Aly, Pegram, Tennessee
Marti Attoun, Joplin, Missouri
Carol Beck-Round, Claremore, Oklahoma
Kathleen Conroy, Victoria, British Columbia, Canada
Vicki Cox, Lebanon, Missouri
Debi Drake, Placerville, California
Veda Eddy, The Villages, Florida
Jackie Sheckler Finch, Bloomington, Indiana
Debbe Geiger, Massapequa, New York
Ann Goebel, Knightdale, North Carolina
Candi Helseth, Minot, North Dakota
Robyn Hoffman, Quitman, Arkansas
Laurel Holliday, Seattle, Washington
Melonee McKinney Hurt, Spring Hill, Tennessee
Warren Hynes, North Plainfield, New Jersey
Leah Ingram, New Hope, Pennsylvania

Elizabeth Johnson, Lansing, Michigan
Karen Karvonen, Englewood, Colorado
Sheryl Kayne, Weston, Connecticut
Carole Marshall, Port Townsend, Washington
Elaine Hobson Miller, Ashville, Alabama
Susan Palmquist, Eden Prairie, Minnesota
Carol Patton, Las Vegas, Nevada
j. poet, San Francisco, California
M. B. Roberts, Hollywood, Florida
Leanna Skarnulis, Austin, Texas
Kathy Summers, Cave Creek, Arizona
Sandy Summers, Charleston, South Carolina
Kristen Tribe, Decatur, Texas
Alice M. Vollmar, Minneapolis, Minnesota
Vivian Wagner, New Concord, Ohio
Diana West, Joplin, Missouri
Kay West, Nashville, Tennessee
Pam Windsor, Louisville, Kentucky

Photo Credits

The following photographers contributed to this book:

David Becker, 212
Gary Bogdon, 174
Russ Bryant, 52
Gary Bublitz, 72
Samuel Castro, 256
Clarke Davis, 126
Joe Duty, 206
Donna Fisher, 108
Jason A. Frizzelle, 34
Gretchen Graham, 198
Brian Griffin, 62
David Grubbs, 250
Mike Gullett, 180, 230
Richman Haire, 132
John Hayes, 56, 202
Andy Heidt, 78

Candi Helseth, 84
Russ Holloway, 6
Stephen Holman, 164
Julianna Hunter, 12
Jason Janik, 138
Taylor Jones, 168
Doug Keese, 192
Ken Klotzbach, 100
Ed Lallo, 66
Joshua Lawton, 244
Courtesy of Life is good, 6
Joshua McCoy, *Bowling Green Daily News,* 46
Courtesy of Helen Myers, 1
David Mudd, 186, 224, 234, 238, 260
Earl Neikirk, 148
Danny Obadia, 90
Michael L. Palmieri, 266
Dale Pickett, 218
Brad Stauffer, 104, 114, 154
Ervan D. Stuewe, 24
Chad Surmick, 120
John Touscany, 40
Alvis Upitis, 142
Doug Wells, 94
Michael Weschler Photography, 18
Peter Wiant, 158

Contact Information for Charities

Learn more about hometown hero efforts described in this book at:

Marilyn Adams's Farm Safety 4 Just Kids:
www.fs4jk.org or (800) 423-5437

Pastor Denny Bellesi's Kingdom Assignment:
www.kingdomassignment.com

John Beltzer's Songs of Love Foundation:
www.songsoflove.org or (800) 960-7664

P. K. Beville's Second Wind Dreams:
www.secondwind.org or (678) 624-0500

The Bookmobile Ladies' Friends of the Bookmobile:
www.geauga.lib.oh.us/GCPL/Friends/BKfriends.htm

Raymond Carver's Living Room Theatre of Salado:
www.lrtsalado.org

Jeanette Cram's Treat the Troops Inc.:
www.treatthetroops.org or (843) 682-3783

Phillip Deason's Moody Miracle League:
www.moodymiracleleague.com;
and the Miracle League Association: www.miracleleague.com

Tynsy Foster's Healing Memory Bears:
www.tynsysmiraclebear.com or (918) 786-8804

Kirt Giovannoni's Manteca Murals:
www.mantecausd.net/MHS or
(209) 825-3150 to book a free group tour

Tiffany Grant's Prom Wishes Inc.: www.prom-wishes-inc.org

Philip Gulley's Harmony: www.philipgulleybooks.com

Barbara Hensley's Hope Chest for Breast Cancer:
www.hopechest.us or (952) 471-8700

Marvin Hume's Sunset Beach Salute:
www.sunsetbeachnj.com/flagceremony.html or (800) 757-6468

Steve Hund Jr.'s stove restoration business:
www.millcreekantiques.com or (785) 636-5520

Dayton O. Hyde's Black Hills Wild Horse Sanctuary:
www.wildmustangs.com or (800) 252-6652

John Rice Irwin's Museum of Appalachia:
www.museumofappalachia.com or (865) 494-7680

Bert and John Jacobs's Life is good® charities:
www.lifeisgood.com/festivals/our-chosen-charities

Pam Koner's Family to Family food pantry:
www.family-to-family.com

Anthony Leanna's Heavenly Hats:
www.heavenlyhats.com or (920) 434-4151, ext. 1400

Lani Malmberg's Ewe4ic Ecological Services: www.goatapelli.com

Robin Maynard's Cheerful Givers birthday foundation:
www.cheerfulgivers.org or call (651) 226-8738

Wilma Melville's National Disaster Search Dog Foundation:
www.ndsdf.org or (888) 459-4376

Hal O'Leary's National Sports Center for the Disabled:
www.nscd.org or (970) 726-1540

Carolyn Reedom's John C. Vanderburg Rainforest Biosphere:
www.mybiosphere.com or (702) 799-0540, ext. 4007

Bob Rowe's Renaissance Enterprises:
www.visioncouncil.org/bobrowe/

Jared and Betsy Saul's pet finding service:
www.petfinder.com

Eleanor Stopps's Jefferson County Admiralty Audubon:
www.admiraltyaudubon.org

Tom Taylor's Great U.S. 50 Yard Sale:
www.route50.com/yardsale.html

Emily Weinberger's Greater New Orleans Youth Orchestra:
www.gnoyo.org
and Emily's website: www.onepersoncanmakeadifference.com

Phil Yeh's Cartoonists Across America:
www.wingedtiger.com or (805) 928-4603

John Zweifel's White House:
www.presidentshalloffame.com or call (352) 394-2836

Acknowledgements

Over the years, we have been sincerely touched by the reactions from our readers to the *Hometown Heroes* features in *American Profile* magazine. "More, more and more!" they would tell us, and we are more than happy to oblige them. This book is simply another way for us to share these heroes with readers like you.

Most importantly, we are grateful to the heroes outlined in this book. Without their passion, sacrifice and belief in something greater than their own personal comfort, we would not have the privilege in bringing these stories to you.

Thanks go to the three project editors who helped bring this book to you: Stuart Englert and Richard McVey, who originally researched, selected and expertly edited these fine stories for inclusion in *American Profile* magazine; and Marta Aldrich, who successfully completed the gargantuan task of selecting the best fifty hero stories for this book, working closely with the writers of the stories to bring them up to date, and editing and organizing it again for you. Her efforts went well beyond the call of duty.

In addition, *American Profile* is fortunate to work with such incredible writers around the country who, in many cases, brought the story ideas to us for consideration. They believed in the people and their stories and knew that the readers of *American Profile* would identify with their "heroic" efforts. Thank you!

Sincere thanks to photo editor David Mudd, whose organization, patience and persistence helped to bring to you the wonderful photos that accompany each story—many taken by him. We are also grateful to the dozens of photographers who took the photographs that are included here for you to enjoy.

Thanks also to executive editor Charlie Cox, who consistently holds to the mission of the magazine, and whose leadership of the editorial group is crucial in putting out a product that is welcomed each week by millions of readers across the United States. We sincerely appreciate the efforts of Kim Cornish here in Franklin, Tennessee, who helped with many of the administrative facets of the project with her usual gracious and efficient manner.

Thanks to Cynthia DiTiberio and her colleagues at HarperSanFrancisco, who believed in this project and completed it in record time, and whose genuine patience helped us carefully craft this final product.

And thanks to you, the reader, for considering this book as part of your collection. We leave you with this simple thought, and may it be true in your life:

Nurture your mind with great thoughts; to believe in the heroic makes heroes.

BENJAMIN DISRAELI (1804–1881)

American Profile Magazine
Franklin, Tennessee
February 2007

Index of Heroes by Last Name

Index by Location

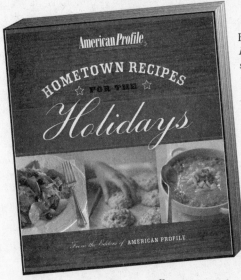